BOURBON,
STRAIGHT

BOURBON, STRAIGHT

The Uncut and Unfiltered Story of
American Whiskey

Charles K. Cowdery

Chicago, Illinois

For information about this book, write or call:
>   Made and Bottled in Kentucky
>   PMB 298, 3712 N. Broadway
>   Chicago, IL 60613-4198
>   773-477-9691
>   cowdery@ix.netcom.com
>   http://cowdery.home.netcom.com

First printing 2004.

ISBN 0-9758703-0-0

Library of Congress Control Number: 2004108280

Contents

Of Sex and Shellfish.

Like sex, alcohol is one of those subjects where much of what people *think* they know is wrong. The similarities do not end there. Both subjects are laden with taboos, not least of which is their unsuitability for children. Perhaps that is the reason for such wide-spread ignorance about both. We don't learn much about them as children and as adults, we don't learn anything very well.

What we do learn about both subjects growing up often is contradictory. Our parents and teachers tell us one thing, our peers tell us something else. Sex education, fortunately, has improved a lot in recent decades. Alcohol education not so much.

One example of this ignorance, of relevance to whiskey fans, is the prejudice against 'hard liquor' embodied in that very expression. Conventional wisdom holds that distilled spirits are a uniquely dangerous form of alcohol, more prone to abuse than beer or wine. People drinking bourbon whiskey for the first time often characterize it as 'strong.' Likewise, many people believe tequila has unique intoxicating qualities more akin to narcotics than alcohol. Absinthe, which is still banned in the United States, has a similar legendary reputation. Certain tropical concoctions using several different rums are considered unusually potent. I say 'prejudice against' but, of course, people seeking intoxication take the opposite view, based on the same erroneous beliefs.

The fact is that alcohol is alcohol and so far as alcohol's intoxicating effect goes, the beverage type is irrelevant. All of the alcohol in alcoholic beverages is ethanol and it is all exactly the same, chemically and functionally, whether it is in wine, beer or tequila. The only thing that matters is the *amount* of alcohol you consume. As someone who attended college at one of the last bastions of 'low beer' (no more than 3.2 percent alcohol by volume), I can certify that it is possible to become severely intoxicated on anything that contains alcohol, even in low concentrations, if you drink enough of it. The level of intoxication a given individual will reach is solely a function of the amount of alcohol consumed, how quickly it is consumed, the body weight of the drinker and the drinker's individual metabolism. The type of beverage (beer, wine, whiskey, vodka, tequila, rum, etc.) has nothing to do with it. The alcohol in white wine is exactly the same as the alcohol in tequila. Alcohol is alcohol, period. The Distilled Spirits Council of the United States (DISCUS), the industry trade group, likes to point out that a typical glass of wine, a typical glass of beer and a typical cocktail all contain about the same amount of alcohol.

I mention this because this is a book about American whiskey and whiskey drinkers are often

unfairly pigeonholed as 'hard drinkers' solely based
on *what* they drink. But if I'm sipping a couple fingers
of Kentucky bourbon and you're pounding glass after
glass of white wine, who is taking in more alcohol? It is
not 'what,' only 'how much' that matters. Part of my
purpose in writing this book is to correct some of these
common misconceptions about alcohol in general and
American straight whiskey in particular.

However, this book is *not* about intoxication,
alcohol abuse, alcoholism or other health-related
matters. About all I intend to say on those subjects I
will say right now. I maintain that everyone who drinks
alcoholic beverages does so, at least in part, for their
intoxicating effect and there is nothing wrong with
enjoying that part of it. I have debated this point with,
in particular, wine drinkers who claim to care only
about taste. I am not convinced. The clincher is when
they say, as they invariably do, that they wish alcohol-
free wines tasted better, because then they would
drink nothing else. Unfortunately, what alcohol-free
wines lack that makes them so unappealing is alcohol.
Without alcohol, it is a different experience. I am not
saying everyone who drinks does so to get drunk. I am
just saying that part of the enjoyment of consuming
alcohol is the psychoactive effect.

As for alcoholism, it is a complicated issue and one
that I am not particularly qualified to discuss. Is it a
medical problem, a moral problem, or both? Is it a
disease, an allergy? Certainly it is similar to an allergy
in that alcoholics should not consume alcohol, just as
people who are allergic to shellfish should eschew
shrimp. When people who should not use alcohol do
use it, bad things happen to them and the people

around them. That said, and hewing to the shellfish analogy, the fact that some people cannot safely metabolize shrimp should not prevent the rest of us from enjoying it.

Where the shellfish analogy breaks down is that people who are allergic to shellfish but consume it anyway seldom hurt anyone but themselves. They don't drive their cars into other people, pick fights with strangers, neglect their family, or do any of the other awful things alcohol abusers do. They also don't have a seemingly irresistible urge to keep eating shellfish even though they know what will happen to them if they do. This makes alcoholism unlike any other allergy. Still, the overwhelming majority of drinkers do none of those bad things and can consume alcohol daily for a lifetime with no ill effects on themselves, their family, or their community. Should that majority be penalized for the failings of a minority? Of course not. Alcohol abuse is a serious matter, both for those afflicted and for society in general. It is a worthy topic, but beyond the scope of this project. That is a different book.

The reason I raise the subject of alcoholism at all is because responsible beverage alcohol enthusiasts often have to deal with neo-prohibitionists who seem determined to spoil our fun. That struggle, I fear, will never be over. Modern anti-alcohol crusaders dress it up as a health issue or a protect-the-children issue but to them it is still really a moral issue. They think alcohol is evil and must be vanquished. Is alcohol a bad thing? Or is it a good thing that some people abuse? Abraham Lincoln laid out that dichotomy in a speech to the Washington Temperance Society of

Springfield, Illinois, in 1842. Being a politician he never really answered the question in his address, but I will give you my opinion. For most people, alcohol is a good thing. From a health standpoint, most research shows that moderate alcohol consumption is healthier than abstinence. The appreciation of fine alcohol products can be as satisfying as any other gastronomical indulgence. And, yes, the high is fun too. As for the issue of children and alcohol, it is much like children and sex. For most people, childhood is not a permanent state. As they progress toward adulthood, children inevitably and appropriately become curious about adult activities. Education that is forthright, tailored to the individual child's level of development, and delivered by a trustworthy adult—preferably the child's parent—is the ideal. Ignorance is the real devil, especially when it is misinformation dished out by zealous busybodies.

I arrived at these conclusions from personal experience. I was raised Roman Catholic, exposed primarily to German and Irish Catholics, and attended Catholic schools. One day in Health class, I think it was in 9th grade, someone from Alcoholics Anonymous made a presentation. Much to our surprise, the speaker wasn't some neutral third party, it was the father of one of our friends. It must have taken tremendous courage to do that, for him and his family, but the effect was powerful and unforgettable. In that community, people drank and didn't feel the need to hide it. We saw the full range of drinking behavior; good, bad and ugly. Even the parish priests could be seen enjoying a beer at the church festival. When we asked questions about alcohol, we generally received straight answers. When we asked for a taste, say at a family party, we usually were directed to ask our parents, but sometimes we got a sip. I had one experience, when I was about six, at a party at my grandparents' home, where more than one partygoer granted me a taste. I got sick. My mother, without being too censorious, explained to me *why* I got sick. It was what parents call a teaching opportunity. I learned my lesson, more or less. For as long as I can remember, my parents always enjoyed a glass of bourbon in the evening before dinner. That was their private time together, away from us kids, when they talked about their respective days. That too was a positive example. As a teenager I experimented with alcohol—and other things—in risky ways that my parents certainly did not endorse, and punished when they caught me, but overall and in the long run I think I learned the right lessons, mostly through good examples.

I hope more than anything that this book will be accepted as a source for reliable information about American whiskey. I have worked hard to make it as accurate as possible. Its title reflects my commitment to 'talk straight' about this subject. Often that has meant cutting through marketing mumbo jumbo, some of which I created in a past life. (I was active on the marketing side of the beverage alcohol industry for about 15 years.)

Seven decades after the repeal of National Prohibition, beverage alcohol continues to be highly regulated and heavily taxed. The very names we use for different products (bourbon, rye, etc.) are regulated by the federal government. Most writings about bourbon begin with the federal regs, but those tell only part of the story. Like any industry, especially any very old one, the whiskey business has a lot of peculiar jargon and practices. I have tried to illuminate those as well.

The appreciation of fine whiskey is an intense sensory experience with a significant cultural component. It is sophisticated in the best sense of the word. There is a lot to it. This book, however, is not an encyclopedia. Several excellent books of that type are already available. This book, based on my more than 20 years of involvement with the American whiskey industry, is more personal and idiosyncratic. It is about the stuff that has fascinated me and made me want to know more. Some of it is based on articles I wrote for my equally personal and idiosyncratic newsletter, *The Bourbon Country Reader.* However, I can assure subscribers to that publication that none of it is a verbatim lift from those pages.

To me, American straight whiskey is a unique and valuable part of American culture, and its heritage is a significant and under-explored part of American history. I hope this book can begin to correct that oversight.

- Chuck Cowdery
June, 2004

And Let's Not Forget...

Let me begin with an apology to anyone I am about to not mention. Sorry about that. This book is the result of working and poking around in the liquor business for more than 20 years. I have known many kind and helpful people through that association, too many to mention here. Too many to even remember.

In some ways, this current project began in 1991, when I proposed the video production that became "Made and Bottled in Kentucky," my documentary about the Kentucky whiskey business. Kentucky Educational Television (KET) and the Kentucky Distillers Association (KDA) funded that project. KET, of course, also broadcast it and distributed it to public television stations throughout the U.S. Thanks are due to Mike White, who told me about the KET grants in the first place and went on to be my videographer and editor, and to the versatile Roger Bondurant, who handled lighting and sound, and produced the music track. Alfred Phillips designed the "Made and Bottled in Kentucky" logo that is doing double duty on the cover of this book. Ed O'Daniel, Executive Director of the KDA, helped me launch the documentary as did Phil Lynch of Brown-Forman and Bill Samuels of Maker's Mark.

In 1994, I began a newsletter about American whiskey called *The Bourbon Country Reader.* I created it to give myself an outlet for my continuing research and writing on the subject. Thanks to everyone who has subscribed over the years for their encouragement of what has often seemed a quixotic endeavor.

Similarly, the members of StraightBourbon.com, an online discussion group in which I have participated since 1999, have kept me interested in this subject and looking into ever darker corners for new tidbits of information. Thanks particularly to Jim Butler, the proprietor.

Others who were helping me with this book project before any of us, including me, knew that's what we were working on include John and Linda Lipman, Mike Veach, Linn Spencer, Gary Regan and Mardee Haidin Regan. Some of my longtime friends in the industry who have always been ready to answer my weird questions include Chris Morris of Brown-Forman; Jimmy Russell of Wild Turkey; Max Shapira, Larry Kass, Parker Beam and Craig Beam of Heaven Hill; Mark Brown of Buffalo Trace; and Sam Cecil, retired but formerly of Maker's Mark. Thanks also to John Hansell, Lew Bryson and Amy Westlake of Malt Advocate Magazine, and Dominic Roskrow of WHISKY Magazine. Flaget Nally and Mary Hite of the Oscar Getz Museum of Whiskey History also were always there when I needed them.

Bettye Jo Boone, who is descended from Jacob Beam via her grandfather, Harry Beam, has been a source for old clippings from the Kentucky Standard, Bardstown's newspaper, as well as the sort of insights only a lifetime resident of that unique community could provide, not to mention her boundless energy and loyal friendship. She also hooked me up with her aunt, Jo Ann Beam, who left us this past January. Aunt Jo was the self-appointed, unofficial Beam family historian, a mission she passed on to Bettye Jo.

Three people who performed a very special duty were Jeff Wade, Gary Gillman and Steve Cowdery, my younger brother. They each read this thing before publication and provided invaluable feedback. Thanks also to Marcella Garza and Erich Harper, who helped with production.

- CKC

Chapter One

The Roots of Bourbon Whiskey in America.

It is February, 1621. The Mayflower colonists are panicked because they are running out of beer. To prevent them from depleting the ship's stores and leaving its crew beer-less for the voyage home, the settlers are "hasted ashore and made to drink water," according to the diary of the colony's future governor. They survive this bold experiment and soon are making their own liquors, using local ingredients when imported barley and hops are unavailable.

Are you surprised to learn that those people we now think of as repressive, sanctimonious Puritans (my nine-times great-grandfather, William Cowdery, among them), who burned witches and branded adulterers, also routinely downed several beers a day? Such was the habit of most Europeans at that time. In the 17th century, alcohol was considered essential for life, much safer than water and good to prevent chills, aid digestion, and strengthen the constitution. As Increase Mather wrote in 1673, "Drink is in itself a good creature of God, and to be received with thankfulness."

But the colonists also felt the need to regulate alcohol sales and use. My paternal line is descended from William Cowdery, who immigrated to the Massachusetts Bay Colony from England in 1630. He was one of the founders of what is now Wakefield, Massachusetts, and served for many years as its town clerk. In 1654, the General Court of Massachusetts "...empowered and ordered..." William, in his official capacity:

> ...to sell wine of any sort, and strong liquors, to the Indians, as to his judgment shall seem most meet and necessary for their relief in just and urgent occasions, and not otherwise, provided he shall not sell or deliver more than one pint to any one Indian at any one time upon any pretence whatever.

He also was authorized to perform marriages, the town being considered "remote from any magistrate, but also destitute of any person empowered to solemnize marriage, the want whereof is the occasion of much trouble and sometimes disappointment."

The foundation for bourbon whiskey was laid in those early years of European settlement. Corn (maize) was unknown in Europe until Columbus but had been cultivated by Native Americans for about 6,500 years. That makes corn the one distinctly American ingredient in New World whiskies. There is an uncorroborated report that a distillery in New York City (then New Amsterdam) made spirits from corn in 1640, just four years after the Dutch settlement there was established. At about that same time, back in Holland, the Dutch were inventing 'jenever,' a name the English subsequently shortened to 'gin.' There is better evidence that at least corn beer (an essential precursor for corn spirits) had been made by 1662, because in that year John Winthrop Jr., the governor of Connecticut, was honored for successfully making it.

Although corn was known, grown, and probably distilled in colonial times, most colonial whiskey was made from rye, a familiar Old World grain. George Washington, after his presidency, had a rye whiskey distillery on his Mt. Vernon plantation that in its time was one of the largest in North America. There were well-established rye whiskey industries in Maryland, Virginia and Pennsylvania before settlers pierced the Appalachians. Even thereafter, the western Pennsylvania distillers who fomented the Whiskey Rebellion were making primarily rye whiskey. During the colonial period and for a long time thereafter, 'whiskey' in America meant a spirit made primarily from rye, although what they called 'Indian corn' was often a secondary ingredient, as was malted barley. Corn as a principal ingredient would not come into its own until the end of the 18th century, after Daniel Boone began to lead settlers through the Cumberland Gap into what is now Kentucky.

In addition to beer and whiskey, early Americans drank cider (i.e., fermented apple juice), applejack (distilled cider), other fruit spirits and rum.

The first European settlers in what was then the western territory of Virginia established Fort Harrod (modern Harrodsburg, Kentucky) in 1774. It is likely that they were also the commonwealth's first distillers.

From the start, they would have distilled corn because that was their principal crop. As they learned from the Indians, corn was a better crop to plant in Kentucky soil than rye, wheat or any other Old World grain because it grew faster, yielded more and required less care. We assume the first distilling happened shortly after the first settlement was established because that is what all early Kentucky settlers did. As soon as they had a surplus of corn—more than they and their livestock could eat—they made the rest into whiskey.

Soon settlers were pouring into Kentucky to plant corn and make whiskey. Some carried small copper pot stills across the mountains, while others rigged up simple contraptions from logs, barrels and whatever pipe they could make or find. These early settlers included Jacob Beam (great-grandfather of Jim Beam), Robert Samuels (ancestor of Marker's Mark president Bill Samuels), Basil Hayden (grandfather of Old Grand-Dad founder R. B. Hayden), Daniel Weller (grandfather of W. L. Weller), and thousands of other farmer-distillers, who came to Kentucky and Tennessee mostly from Pennsylvania, Maryland and Virginia. The Kentucky territory grew fast. In just sixteen years, Kentucky's population grew from nothing to 73,000. In 1792, Kentucky became the 15th state.

It is often written that resistance to the 1791 excise tax on spirits, which led to the Whiskey Rebellion, prompted many western Pennsylvania distillers to move to Kentucky. This seems to be more legend than fact. True, the tax was widely despised in western Pennsylvania. President Washington even had to march an army there in 1794 to quell the unrest. But the excise tax was just as unpopular in Kentucky and

Tennessee. Distillers throughout the western frontier resented the tax for many reasons. Two big ones were that it was due when the spirit was produced, not after the whiskey was sold, and it had to be paid in cash. On the frontier, most transactions were barter and cash was scarce. In fact, the medium of exchange that functioned most like a currency was whiskey itself. Some of the distillers offered to pay their taxes in whiskey but they were rebuffed. A similar solution was eventually implemented as the government became a customer for frontier whiskey. The government bought frontier whiskey to give to its soldiers for their daily spirits ration and that provided the distillers with cash for their tax payments.

If anyone came to Kentucky hoping for weaker excise tax enforcement, they were disappointed. Kentucky was no safe haven. Between 1794 and 1800, 177 Kentucky distillers were caught, convicted and fined for violations of the tax law. The tax was repealed in 1802, briefly reinstated from 1814 through 1817, then abolished until 1862, when it was justified by the need to fund the Civil War. Tax or no tax, corn farmers who wanted to take advantage of rapidly growing trade opportunities had to convert their grain into whiskey because that is what could be sold, either locally or loaded onto flat boats and floated down to New Orleans.

When talking about pioneer whiskey-makers, the term farmer-distiller is often used because few if any of these early settlers were solely distillers. As farmers on a frontier, they had to be self-sufficient. Making whiskey was a normal farm chore, as common as smoking hams, weaving cloth or baking bread. It was a way to preserve surplus grain and add value to an agricultural commodity. Only in the mid-19th century did whiskey-making become a vocation in its own right, separate from farming. In 1800, whiskey and tobacco surpassed flour as the principal export crops from the region. It was that export trade that would give bourbon whiskey its name.

Chapter Two

What Is Whiskey? (The Basics)

Whiskey is an alcoholic beverage made by distilling a fermented mash of grain. Whiskey has just three ingredients: grain, water and yeast, the same three ingredients as bread. In North America, the principal grain used is corn (maize), in combination with malted barley, rye or wheat. In Scotland, Ireland, and Japan barley—malted and unmalted—is dominant, although corn and wheat are used there as well.

In the United States, whiskey is defined by law as a grain spirit distilled at less than 190 degrees of proof (95 percent alcohol by volume). Grain spirits distilled at 190 proof and higher are deemed to be neutral, "without distinctive character, aroma, taste, or color." The trade term for this product is 'grain neutral spirits' or GNS. Although it is almost impossible to convince a vodka drinker of this fact, vodka is nothing more than GNS and water, which is added to reduce it from 190+ proof to between 80 and 100 proof for sale. If you want to pick a fight with a vodka drinker, review these facts.

Vodka, by law, has no "distinctive character, aroma, taste, or color." Therefore, what is the difference between the contents of a $10 bottle of vodka and a $50 bottle of vodka? The water? There are differences among vodkas, but some are so subtle as to verge on the imaginary.

Other common beverage products made from GNS are gin and liqueurs. Gin is vodka plus some flavorings, extract of juniper berry primarily. Most liqueurs are vodka mixed with flavorings from fruit, spices or herbs, and usually a sweetener. GNS also is used in many medicines—the popular cold remedy Nyquil is 10 percent alcohol, as much as some liqueurs. GNS also has many industrial uses.

For a product with only three ingredients, the process of making whiskey is surprisingly complicated. The first ingredient, grain, comes to the distillery by the truckload. Whiskey ad writers often tell you how their product uses "only the finest grains," but grain is really a commodity. All of the distilleries use U.S. No. 2 grade corn and similar standard issue rye and wheat. They all buy from the same suppliers. They inspect the grain before they accept it, primarily to avoid mold. All of the distilleries buy malted barley from commercial maltsters. None do their own malting. They do perform their own milling, taking the grain to the consistency of meal. Mills—one for each grain type—are built into the system so grain is milled as needed, just before it is cooked. This design is an obstacle to something whiskey enthusiasts often talk about: four-grain bourbon using both wheat and rye. Every American whiskey distillery is designed to process three different grains, but not four.

The next step is cooking the grain. Americans are the only whiskey-makers who mix several different grains together at this stage. The others make single grain whiskies and combine them after they have been distilled. Cooking is done in a big tank with motorized paddles that keep the mixture from congealing. In some plants, this is done under pressure. The corn meal, mixed with water, is cooked first at the highest temperature. The temperature is then lowered and a flavor grain is added, either rye or wheat. The temperature is lowered again and barley malt is added. Malt does not contribute significantly to the flavor but is used because malting (the process of allowing a grain to germinate, then halting the germination through heat) produces enzymes that convert starch into sugar. Some distillers use commercially prepared enzymes in addition to malt for more efficient conversion.

The product of the cooking and conversion process is known as the mash. Outside of North America, the liquid and solid components of the mash are separated at this stage and only the sugar-rich liquid, called the wort, goes on to the fermentation tanks. In North America the entire mash, solids included, goes through fermentation and on into the still. There are several reasons for this difference but the main effect is that there are more sources of flavor in the North American system.

Distilleries use a lot of water and the fuss people make about the water resources in Kentucky and Tennessee is legitimate. The important fact is that the water there is naturally filtered through limestone—specifically blue limestone of the Lower Silurian of the

Trenton period. The limestone adds calcium and removes iron salts, both of which make it favorable to yeast. Some distilleries use water from their own springs while a few use 'city water.' Some use 'city water' for things like cooling and cleaning, but only spring water goes into the whiskey. All of the distilleries do some additional filtering and processing of the water, regardless of its source. Good water is absolutely crucial. That is not hype.

A distillery is a maze of pipes and pumps used for moving the product from one location to the next. In a bourbon distillery, the substance that moves from the mash tubs to the fermenters and from there to the still is a semi-solid slurry that looks and feels like watery oatmeal. Fermentation is the process common to all alcoholic beverages. When fruit juice is fermented we call it wine, when cooked grains are fermented we call it beer. The fermenters in an American whiskey distillery are big tanks, usually open but sometimes enclosed. The old ones are made of cypress, the new ones are stainless steel. As new mash enters the fermenter, spent mash from the most recent distillation is being pumped in as well. This is the famous sour mash process. Spent mash is also called slop, because historically this by-product was fed to pigs and cattle who were kept on the distillery premises for that purpose. It is also called backset, or setback, a reference to its function in the sour mash process. Whatever you call it—spent mash, spent beer, slop, stillage, backset or setback—it is what comes out of the still at the end of the distillation process, after virtually all of the alcohol has been extracted from it. As much as one-quarter of the mash in a fermenter will be backset, although each distiller has a different formula. Backset gives the mash a slightly sour taste, hence the term 'sour mash.' The use of backset assures that the Ph of the mash will be uniform from batch to batch, creating an ideal environment for the yeast. Today, this could be controlled by other means, but sour mash is an important part of the heritage and every American whiskey distiller uses it.

At this point the third and final ingredient, yeast, is added. Yeast is a microorganism that consumes sugar and excretes alcohol and carbon dioxide. The process is energetic and also produces heat. Yeast spores are everywhere and not all yeast is the same. Some yeast strains are good for making whiskey and some are not. The yeast strain used is a significant contributor to the flavor of the beverage. Distillers control their yeasts very carefully and knowing how to handle yeast is a big part of being a distiller. In a 1936 magazine article about Kentucky's top distillers, their full job description was usually given as 'distiller and yeast maker.' Fermenting a whiskey mash isn't very much different than fermenting beer or wine. It takes several days and its speed can be tempered by cooling the liquid. This is done by pumping cold water into pipes that line the fermentation tubs. When the alcohol level reaches about 11 percent it begins to poison the yeast and they die off, which completes the fermentation. Yes, the yeast are poisoned by their own waste. The environmentalist symbolism is poignant.

The next stop for the product, now called 'distiller's beer,' is the still. Although any grain spirit distilled at less than 190 proof can legally be called whiskey, it must come off the still at less than 160 proof (80 percent alcohol) to be called bourbon whiskey, rye whiskey, wheat whiskey, malt whiskey, or rye malt whiskey. High proof whiskey (between 160 and 190 proof) is not sold as such but is an ingredient of blended whiskey. Since flavor is inversely proportional to proof, whisky-makers who want to preserve even more of the flavor present in their fermented mash will distill out at a proof below the legal maximum of 160, the lowest being about 110. Distillation is based on the fact that alcohol vaporizes at a lower temperature than water so if you heat a fermented liquid to just the right temperature, the alcohol will vaporize and most of the water will stay behind. That vapor, when subsequently condensed back into a liquid, will have a much higher concentration of alcohol.

Whiskey is usually distilled twice. The first distillation is done in a column still, called the beer still. It is a round shaft about three feet in diameter and two stories high. Its insides are copper and stainless steel. Beer enters at the top, steam rises from the bottom. A succession of perforated, stainless steel plates impedes the progress of the beer as gravity pulls it down through the column, giving the steam time to capture and carry away the spirit. The alcohol-laden vapor is drawn off and quickly condensed into a clear, potent liquid called 'low wines.' This liquid goes into a second, alembic-style still, known as a doubler. (Some use a variation, called a thumper, because it uses steam which makes a thumping sound as it is introduced. The standard doubler uses direct heat.) The second distillation increases the alcohol concentration even more—up to the desired proof—and the result is called 'high wines.' Various adjustments in both of these stills determine the final distillation proof as well as the flavor of the distillate.

The term 'proof' comes from a time when frontier distillers using primitive stills were lucky to achieve 50 percent alcohol. Various crude methods were used to determine the alcohol content of distilled beverages being offered for sale. Spirits that passed these tests were considered 'proved' or 'proof goods.' When measurement techniques improved, 50 percent alcohol was still considered the standard and was thereafter referred to as '100 proof.' Proof is stated in degrees and is often written using the same symbol, a superscripted circle, used for stating temperature (e.g., 100°). I have always found this awkward and don't use it, preferring to just spell out the word 'proof' instead.

Proof is always the percentage of alcohol by volume doubled. Since percentage of alcohol is really the point, and since product labels now all state percentage of alcohol by volume, expressing it in degrees of proof is redundant. So why is it still done? Because it is traditional and this is an industry in which heritage is important, as you may already have noticed.

Since alcohol is alcohol and alcohol all tastes the same (again, try convincing a vodka drinker of this), it is the *non*-alcohol components of a distillate that convey its distinctive flavor characteristics. These non-alcohol by-products of the distillation process include various fusel oils and acids, and are known as congeners. Although congeners give whiskey, brandy, rum, tequila and other non-neutral spirits their distinctive flavor characteristics, their presence has not always been considered desirable. Some congeners have an unpleasant odor and taste, and can be poisonous at high levels. In all distilling cultures, the quest has been to tame or remove the congeners and thereby make the beverage more palatable. Some early distillers chose to mask undesirable odors and flavors with herbs, berries, spices, fruit, and other pleasant flavors. Those spirits were the ancestors of today's flavored vodkas, gins, bitters, schnapps and aquavits. Other distillers discovered the benefits of filtering new distillate through charcoal or bone dust, aging it in wood, or both. As distilling technology improved, it became possible to strip the spirit of all or virtually all of its congeners by simply distilling it out at a very high proof. This is the quest of most vodka makers and is what they mean when they talk about purity. In other words, "purity" equals "neutrality," i.e., flavorlessness. With whiskey, brandy and other spirits you want to retain the flavor of the original ingredients, so the trick is to eliminate or tame 'bad' congeners while preserving 'good' ones. This is done through multiple distillation, through the design of the stills themselves, and through filtering and aging.

Today, most whiskey is aged in oak barrels before it is bottled and sold. To be called *bourbon* whiskey (or rye, wheat, malt, or rye malt whiskey) it must be reduced with water to less than 125 proof (if it was distilled higher than that, as most is) and stored in new oak barrels that have been charred on the inside. To be called *straight* whiskey, it must remain in those barrels for at least two years. Whiskey that has not been aged is called green whiskey or white dog and is as clear as vodka. Corn whiskey is the only example of green whiskey that a consumer may buy. 'Georgia Moon' is the most popular brand of corn whiskey. Green bourbon mash whiskey is used as blending stock for American blended whiskies such as Seagram's Seven Crown.

Aged whiskey gets its reddish-brown color and much of its flavor from the new charred oak barrel. The aging process works like this. During warm weather, the whiskey expands into the wood. During cool weather (or even during the cool evening of the same day), the liquid contracts, pulling itself back out of the wood and bringing with it various sugars, tannins and other flavors. The char through which the whiskey passes during these aging cycles helps tame the congeners. This is the short version, aging has its own chapter later.

Unlike wine, whiskey does all of its aging in the barrel. Although this is generally accepted, a few distillers contend that small changes may occur after bottling, but for the most part bottled whiskey does not change, certainly not the way wine does. Wine in the bottle can improve but it can also spoil. The bacteria that can turn wine into vinegar are powerless against whiskey because of its high alcohol content.

Although two years of aging is the legal minimum for straight whiskies such as bourbon, four to six years is typical for a standard bourbon or rye and many of the better products are aged for eight years or more. Because American straight whiskies (bourbon, rye, Tennessee) are always aged in *new,* charred barrels, it is possible to over-age them. After about 12 years, the spirit may begin to be too woody for most tastes, although there are some very fine bourbons marketed at as much as 23 years. One factor that pushes distillers to age their product for at least four years is the legal requirement that younger whiskey must reveal its age somewhere on the label. You might have to hunt for it, but it will be there, probably stated in months (e.g., 'thirty-six months' instead of '3 years.') If there is no age statement on the label then you know the whiskey is at least 4 years old and probably not much older. Many of the top selling brands such as Jack Daniel's, Wild Turkey and Maker's Mark fall into this category.

Two of the most popular products in the bourbon category—Jack Daniel's and George Dickel—are not bourbons at all. They are Tennessee whiskey. For the most part this can be regarded as a technicality. Although 'Tennessee whiskey' does not appear in the federal regulations that define 'straight bourbon' and 'straight rye,' it is very similar to bourbon and generally considered a straight whiskey even though it technically is not one. Two factors make Tennessee whiskey distinct. The obvious one is that it must be made in Tennessee. The other is that the whiskey is run through a charcoal filtration column 10 feet thick before it goes into the barrel. This quickly leaches out some of the undesirable congeners and jump-starts the aging process. Distillers on either side of the Kentucky-Tennessee border will argue until the end of time about whether this improves or ruins the whiskey.

Early Times exists in a similar regulatory limbo. It calls itself 'Kentucky whiskey' and adheres to all the regulations for 'straight bourbon' except whiskey aged in used barrels is mixed with whiskey aged in new barrels in a ratio of 1:4.

The other major types of straight whiskey are straight rye and straight corn. In a straight rye whiskey, rye must be at least 51 percent of the grain mash bill. The rest can be anything but usually it is corn, along with the ubiquitous 5 to 10 percent malt. In the regulations, bourbon stands in relationship to rye where corn logically ought to be (i.e., more than 51 percent of the mash for bourbon must be corn). Consequently, straight corn whiskey must be at least 80 percent corn. Old Charter bourbon, which is more than 80 percent corn, can call itself either straight bourbon or straight corn. Old Charter aside, only one distillery makes straight corn whiskey for sale as such (others may make it for blending stock). In contrast, six distilleries make straight rye including one— Anchor—that uses 100 percent malted rye. Tennessee whiskey and Kentucky whiskey mash bills are the same as bourbon mash bills, i.e., mostly corn, though that is true as a matter of custom, not law.

Although Canadian whisky is often referred to as 'rye,' few Canadian whiskies have rye as their primary ingredient. The primary grain in Canadian whisky is corn, but most of the corn whiskey used is distilled at a very high proof (though less than 190) to nearly neutralize its flavor. This is used as a base whiskey, to which one or several very flavorful lower proof whiskies are added. The lower proof 'flavoring' whiskey may be made from any grain, but rye is the signature flavor in most Canadian whiskies. Even so, a U.S. straight rye will be made with considerably more rye grain than most Canadian whiskies.

The exclusive use of *new* charred barrels is one of the key differences between whiskey made in the

United States and whiskey made elsewhere. Scottish, Irish, Canadian and Japanese distillers reuse their barrels many times, literally until they fall apart. Those countries are where most used bourbon barrels go. Because used barrels are, well, *used*, whiskies aged in them benefit less from short aging and more from extended aging, which is why you will see a lot of 25-year-old scotch but very little 25-year-old bourbon.

Another American whiskey term you may come across is 'bonded' or 'bottled-in-bond.' This is another term that comes from the federal regulations. A bottled-in-bond straight whiskey must be the product of one distillation season and one distiller at one distillery. It is aged at least four years and bottled at at least 100 proof.

'Small batch' and 'single barrel' are two fairly recent terms that are not found in the federal regulations. The Jim Beam Brands Company coined the term 'small batch,' but other companies now use it too. It sounds like the whiskey is all handmade in small batches, but it isn't. It comes off the same, big still as everything else, is barreled the same and aged in the same rackhouses. The batch only gets small when the barrels are selected, dumped and bottled. Which is not to say the term is completely illegitimate. Jim Beam's Knob Creek is the most successful 'small batch' bourbon. It is nine years old and 100 proof. Not everyone cares about a nine-year-old, 100 proof bourbon, but a few of us do so Jim Beam is nice enough to bottle some up for us. Compared to the volume of their Jim Beam white label, Knob Creek is very 'small batch' indeed.

The term 'single barrel' is a little more meaningful. It means that all of the whiskey in a given bottle came from one barrel, as opposed to the usual practice of dumping many barrels into a big tank before bottling. The significance of this is that the 'big tank' system gives a distiller the opportunity to adjust the whiskey before bottling it, by adding more barrels with qualities the mixture may lack currently. With single barrel bottlings, such adjustments are not possible, so those barrels have to be selected very carefully. Bonded whiskies are the same way. Because they must come from one distillery during one distilling season, you can't improve an immature whiskey by adding a barrel or two of older stock.

In addition to straights, the other big whiskey category is blends, whether they be American, Canadian, Irish, Scottish or Japanese. The Canadian, Irish, Scottish and Japanese blends are always mixtures of aged whiskey, though a large percentage of the blend may be a nearly neutral base whiskey. Flavorings and colorings may also be added.

American blended whiskey, on the other hand, typically contains very little aged whiskey. By law, only 20 percent of the blend must be 100 proof straight whiskey. Some products may contain a little more. The rest is high proof green whiskey, neutral spirits, flavorings, colorings and water. In the United States, the terms 'straight whiskey' and 'blended whiskey' were much fought-over in the late-19th and early-20th centuries. As such, they are terms of art, with formal definitions enshrined in law that don't necessarily correspond to the common meanings of the words. For example, American blended whiskey can contain ingredients that are not whiskey, such as GNS and caramel coloring, and straight whiskey can actually be a combination (i.e., a blend) of straight whiskies of the same type from different distilleries and years.

The rest of the world does not use the term 'straight whiskey.' Until about 30 years ago, it didn't apply because the world's other whiskies were all blends. Then Scotland's distillers started to actively market something called 'single malts' outside of Scotland. The Irish and Japanese followed suit. None of them stopped selling blends but today only Canada sells blends exclusively.

'Single' means the whiskey is entirely the product of one distillery. 'Single malt' generally means a whiskey made entirely from malted barley, although San Francisco's Anchor Distilling makes a single malt from rye. American distilleries seldom use the term 'single' and it is often said that American straights are the same as Scottish singles, but that is not quite accurate. An American straight is more like a vatted malt and an American bond is more like a single.

Although U.S. law governs the labeling of products sold in the U.S., whether made here or imported, the United States is also party to several international treaties regulating the use of terms that refer to a nation's 'distinctive products,' including distilled spirits. In 1993, Canada, Mexico and the U.S. agreed, as part of the North American Free Trade Agreement (NAFTA), to give mutual recognition to distilled spirits products distinctive to each country. In 1994, the foreign ministers of the European Union (EU) approved a similar agreement with the United States to prevent transatlantic competitors from using any of the protected names for locally produced spirits. Article 313 of NAFTA states: "For purposes of standards and labeling, ...the Parties shall recognize Bourbon Whiskey and Tennessee Whiskey as distinctive products of the United States, Canadian Whiskey as a distinctive product of Canada, and Tequila and Mezcal as distinctive products of Mexico." The EU agreement protects their Scotch whisky, Irish whiskey, and Cognac, Armagnac, Calvados and Jerez brandy while protecting our Bourbon Whiskey and Tennessee Whiskey. Italy and Greece opposed the agreement because it failed to protect grappa and ouzo.

The word 'whiskey' comes from an ancient Gaelic expression meaning 'water of life.' In several other languages, the term for a distilled beverage has that same translation (e.g., aquavit, eau de vie). Use of the English word 'whiskey' dates back to the Middle Ages. Today, the spelling 'whiskey' is favored in the U.S. and Ireland, while the 'e' is omitted in Scotland, Canada and Japan. A small number of U.S. makers also spell it without the 'e.'

Chapter Three

How Bourbon Whiskey Got Its Name.

Most of the world's whiskey styles have straightforward names that describe their place of origin. The whisky made in Scotland by Scots is called scotch. The whiskies made in Ireland and Canada, respectively, are called Irish and Canadian. Even bourbon's closest relatives, Tennessee Whiskey and rye, have names that frankly describe either their place of manufacture or principal ingredient, both completely logical naming approaches. So why is America's best known and most popular whiskey style called bourbon, a name borrowed from French royalty? The French, after all, don't even make whiskey.

Most writers who try to unravel this puzzle get it wrong. Here is a typical example, from Alexis Lichine's *New Encyclopedia of Wines & Spirits:*

> Early in the colonial history of America, a Baptist minister, Elijah Craig, established a still in Georgetown, Kentucky and began producing whiskey from a base of corn. The still is said to have been one of the first in Kentucky and

customers in neighboring towns christened his product Bourbon County Whiskey, from the county of origin.

Here is another example, from *A Concise Encyclopedia of Gastronomy,* by Andre L. Simon:

> The name is due to the fact that the first whisky distilled in Kentucky was obtained from ground maize at the mill of one Elijah Craig, in Georgetown, Bourbon County. It was called Bourbon County Whisky at first, and the name Bourbon Whisky has been used ever since for whisky distilled wholly or chiefly from maize.

Even Robert A. Powell, author of a history text used in Kentucky's public schools, repeats this standard but inaccurate explanation. Under 'Bourbon County' in his book *120 Kentucky Counties,* he asserts: "The same name was later given to a pioneer product, Kentucky's famous 'bourbon' whiskey, which was first distilled in this county."

The problem with all these explanations is that they are wrong, or at least not quite right. Because they have been repeated so many times over the years, it never even occurs to anyone to doubt them. Few people in Kentucky, even in the distilling industry, know the true explanation, although it is neither obscure nor difficult to understand. It is, however, slightly more complicated than the standard, but mistaken, tale.

First, let's get the whole Elijah Craig business out of the way. The durable claim that Elijah Craig, a Baptist minister, made the first bourbon whiskey can be traced to Richard Collins, whose *History of Kentucky* was published in 1874. Collins does not identify Craig by name, but writes that "the first Bourbon Whiskey was made in 1789, at Georgetown, at the fulling mill at the Royal spring." This claim is included, without elaboration, on a densely-packed page of short statements under the heading 'Kentucky firsts.' Collins does not attempt to substantiate the claim nor has any evidence ever been produced to support it. Craig was a real person—a major character in early Kentucky history—and he was a distiller. He also operated a fulling mill at the Royal Spring in 1789, so there is little doubt that Collins intended to attribute this milestone to Craig. What is lacking is any evidence that Craig's whiskey was unique in its day, that it alone had somehow been elevated from the raw, green, corn distillate made throughout the frontier to the bourbon whiskey we know today.

In addition to a lack of any evidence to support the Collins claim, which was made almost 100 years after the fact, there is another, more significant problem about connecting the Craig claim to bourbon's name. *Craig's distilling operation was never in Bourbon County,* even with the shifting of county boundaries that took place during Kentucky's early history. Craig didn't move, but the boundaries did as new, smaller counties were created from older and larger ones. Craig's site was first in Fayette County (1780), then Woodford (1788), then Scott (1792). It was *never* in Bourbon County. In addition to making cloth (which is what a fulling mill does) and whiskey, Craig established a school that is today's Georgetown College in Georgetown, Kentucky, the seat of Scott County. Elijah Craig was a remarkable frontier character, but he was not the father of bourbon.

In Elijah Craig's day, making whiskey was commonplace, universally viewed as an economic and personal necessity. It was only much later, in Collins' time, that making and consuming whiskey became controversial. Collins himself sympathized with the prohibitionists who would eventually outlaw whiskey, but distillers and their supporters were quick to embrace his assertion that bourbon was 'invented' by a respected Baptist preacher. This does not explain why Collins attributed the invention of bourbon to Craig, but it does explain why that legend has endured.

So how *did* Kentucky's corn-based whiskey come to be called bourbon? There is a connection with Bourbon County, but it is not what everyone thinks it is.

At the conclusion of the American Revolution, what is now Kentucky was still the Kentucky District of Virginia. Because America was grateful to France for helping us defeat England, the Virginia legislature dropped a number of French names onto American soil. When Virginia began to carve Kentucky into smaller units beginning in 1780, it chose the name of a famous French general for one of the three new counties it created, Fayette. Another early county, created by slicing off a piece of Fayette, was named in honor of the French royal family, the Bourbons. Bourbon County, Virginia, was established in 1785. This brought the number of counties in the vast western territory to five. The Kentucky towns of Louisville, Versailles and Paris were also named during this fit of Francophilia.

By the time Bourbon County was formed in 1785, there already were dozens if not hundreds of small farmer-distillers throughout the region making corn whiskey. In those days, with few roads and limited local markets for farm products, the only practical way for farmers to sell their corn was by first distilling it into whiskey. If they did not have a still, they found a neighbor who did and traded some percentage of the output (typically five to ten percent) as payment for the distilling services. Although it was not practical to transport corn overland to eastern markets, it was practical to transport corn whiskey in this way. Corn whiskey, along with Kentucky's other main export products—flour, tobacco and hemp—also was loaded onto flatboats and shipped via the Ohio River to New Orleans for sale, when the Spanish masters of that city permitted such trade. The first important Ohio River port in Kentucky was at Maysville, which was then called Limestone. Although we don't know exactly when it was established, we know that port was already in use in 1784 when the Virginia legislature assigned "two naval officers or collectors" to the Falls of Ohio (now Louisville) and the "mouth of Limestone" to supervise river traffic and collect tolls.

The port of Limestone served all of Bourbon County, which was then a vast region that included virtually all of modern Kentucky north, east and southeast of Lexington. In 1789, Limestone and the rest of northeastern Bourbon County became Mason County. After Kentucky became a state in 1792, many more new counties were carved from the original Bourbon County and Bourbon County itself shrank to its current modest size. Thirty-four modern Kentucky counties were once part of Bourbon. Because of that common heritage, until about 1820 the entire region continued to be known popularly as 'Old Bourbon.'

During this same period, whiskey became the region's most important export. Because most people living there still called the whole region 'Old Bourbon,' any whiskey shipped from Limestone was invariably advertised and identified on barrelheads as 'Old Bourbon Whiskey,' no matter where it was actually made. In the region, at least, everyone understood the term as simply identifying where the whiskey originated generally, i.e., somewhere in the region known as 'Old Bourbon.' More specifically, it meant any whiskey shipped to market from the port of 'Old Bourbon' at Limestone.

Eventually, this habit of referring to the whole region as 'Old Bourbon' died out and people unfamiliar with the practice began to assume that the word 'old' in the phrase 'Old Bourbon Whiskey' must have referred to the age of the spirits, and that 'Bourbon' must refer to the then much-diminished county of that name. It never referred to either. For one thing, the routine aging of Kentucky whiskey was still several decades in the future.

What made the whiskey from 'Old Bourbon' unique was its principal ingredient: corn. Most of the downriver customers for 'Old Bourbon Whiskey' were tasting corn whiskey for the first time, since most domestic whiskey then was made from rye. Many liked this new style of whiskey and clamored for more, asking for it by name. Recognizing a good thing and showing the initiative that has made American marketing what it is today, other whiskey producers in other parts of Kentucky and adjacent states simply appropriated the name for their own corn whiskey. They began to label their barrels 'Bourbon Whiskey' too, even if it wasn't shipped from Limestone or made within the borders of 'Old Bourbon' County.

Other factors may have facilitated the adoption of 'bourbon' as the generic term for any corn-based whiskey. The eventual market for the product, New Orleans, had a sizable French population that may have liked the French name. In New Orleans for most of the 19th century, brandy imported from France— specifically Cognac—was considered the pinnacle of the distiller's art. Corn whiskey was sweet like Cognac and eventually would be aged in charred oak barrels, like Cognac. A French-sounding name was another way of positioning bourbon whiskey as the 'poor man's Cognac.' Louisville and Shippingport, two early settlements at the Falls of the Ohio, also had large French populations in those early years. Many of these settlers were loyal royalists fleeing the French Revolution (1789). The Falls is the only non-navigable part of the Ohio, so goods shipped down the river had to be unloaded there and portaged around the Falls. The French influence at this important trans-shipment point may also have favored the name. Eventually, all whiskey made primarily from corn was called bourbon to distinguish it from rye-based whiskey.

Today, 'bourbon' has a specific legal meaning that has nothing to do with where it is made. Unlike Tennessee whiskey, which must be made in Tennessee, Bourbon may be made anywhere in the United States. There never has been a legal require- ment that bourbon be made in Kentucky, which is why most Kentucky producers call their product *Kentucky* Bourbon. At one time, Peoria, Illinois, produced a lot of bourbon. Today, there are very few examples of non-

Kentucky bourbon left, Virginia Gentleman being the best known.

So, a short version of how bourbon whiskey was named might go like this: When the American frontier moved west of the Allegheny Mountains, late in the 18th century, whiskey for the first time was made from native corn, or maize. In 1785, a large portion of this new territory was named Bourbon County, after the French royal family. When Bourbon was divided into smaller counties, the region continued to be known as 'Old Bourbon' and corn whiskey made there came to be known as 'Old Bourbon Whiskey.' Eventually, the name 'bourbon' was used to distinguish all American whiskey made principally from corn, regardless of where it was made.

Chapter Four

The New Oak Barrel; Whiskey's Best Friend.

American straight whiskey is unique in several ways, but one of the most significant is the use of new, charred oak barrels to age the spirit. Virtually all whiskies are aged in wood, but only American straight whiskies are aged exclusively in new charred barrels. As a result of this profligacy, slightly used barrels are a major byproduct of American whiskey-making. In Kentucky, you see a lot of flower boxes, furniture and other objects made from old whiskey barrels. There was a time when distilleries gave them away. Now they mostly sell them to distillers in other lands, because the remainder of the world ages its spirits in used cooperage, and virtually all of it is used bourbon barrels.

The knowledge that time in oak containers improves the taste of wine, ale, dairy products and other foods dates back to antiquity. The discovery probably was made not long after the development of strong iron tools made it possible to fashion suitable containers from hard wood. Oak vessels in England, where ale was already the national drink, date from at least the 4th century A.D. It also has long been known (though perhaps not as well understood) that carbon has a beneficial effect on the taste of alcoholic beverages. The word 'toast,' as in 'to drink a toast,' is derived from the ancient custom of flavoring wine and ale by dunking spiced, toasted bread into it.

So when farmer-distillers migrated west in the decades after 1774, some of them probably knew that oak aging improves the flavor of whiskey. Some even knew that charring the wood would improve the taste even more. In those days, most whiskey was not aged, but not for lack of knowledge about the beneficial effects. Frontier whiskey was not aged because it sold just fine in its raw, green condition, straight from the still. One custom was to add a little sugar to make it more palatable, but most people were content to drink it just as it was.

Because whiskey was the virtual currency of frontier America, we have many records of transactions involving it, including offers of sale written in private letters and printed in newspaper advertisements. Since advertising always makes a product sound as good as possible, we can be sure that when aged whiskey was available, it was advertised as such. Sure enough, as early as 1793 'old whiskey' appears in some advertisements, offered at a premium price. By 1814, sellers were announcing the age of their old whiskey in years, although 'common' (i.e., green) whiskey still predominated. It was probably at about this time, or a little later, that the Kentucky innovation of aging whiskey in new, charred oak barrels began. We know that charring itself was nothing new. Barrels were used to hold everything from fish to nails, and when they were empty they usually were used again. Firing the inside of the barrel was an effective way to sterilize it and eliminate any residual flavors left over from its previous contents. However, since charring weakened the wood and thereby shortened a barrel's useful life, this was only done when absolutely necessary.

The first innovation, then, was charring new barrels intended for aging whiskey before their first use. This may have been nothing more than a maturation of both industries. When distilling capacity increased to the point where distillers were able to make more whiskey than they could sell right away, they started to age some, with the idea that they could profit by selling the tastier product later for a higher price. Whiskey merchants also set some of their stock aside for aging and may have been more responsible for the practice initially than were the distillers. Since whiskey aging took barrels out of circulation for a long time, the cooperage industry was forced to increase its production capacity, so more and more of the barrels coming into service were new and made specifically for whiskey aging. Charring used barrels before storing whiskey in them may have become so common, and the benefits so well known, that new barrels intended for whiskey storage were routinely charred too. The fact that no record has been found to show that a radical change in the common practice occurred indicates that whatever changes took place probably were evolutionary.

So the truly important innovation wasn't the decision to char new barrels, it was the decision to discard barrels after a single use. Again, the explanation for this is not too hard to figure out. It may not have been a 'decision' at all. Since whiskey was sold in the barrel, disposing of empties was not the whiskey-maker's problem. Used barrels were a commodity and an owner of one likely could find a use for it closer to home than the distillery where it originated. It also would not have taken long for whiskey makers and whiskey drinkers to recognize the difference between whiskey aged in new barrels and whiskey aged in refilled wood. The prevailing preference must have been for whiskey aged in new wood because that became the most common style.

One characteristic of whiskey aged in new charred barrels is that it gains a distinctive red-amber color, while whiskey aged in used or uncharred barrels is much lighter and more yellow in color. This is how we know approximately when the practice started. The earliest reference we have to Kentucky whiskey being red comes from a letter written in 1849 by a Kentucky politician. The whiskey he describes is attributed to Dr. James C. Crow, who is believed to have been the first bourbon maker to sell no common whiskey, only mature goods.

Another early reference to whiskey being red comes from literature. In *Moby Dick* by Herman Melville, published in 1851, whale blood is compared to certain whiskies of the day:

> "That drove the spigot out of him!" cried Stubb.
> "'Tis July's immortal Fourth; all fountains must run
> wine today! Would now, it were old Orleans
> whiskey, or old Ohio, or unspeakable old
> Monongahela! Then, Tashtego, lad, I'd have ye
> hold a canakin to the jet, and we'd drink round it!
> Yea, verily, hearts alive, we'd brew choice punch
> in the spread of his spout-hole there, and from
> that live punch-bowl quaff the living stuff."

Since this gruesome reference is made without further
explanation, Melville must have been confident that his
readers were familiar enough with red whiskey to
understand the allusion.

When whiskey is stored in a new, charred oak
barrel it gradually soaks into the wood, passing
through the char into a 'red layer' of partially-
caramelized sugars just beneath it. On the far side of
this red layer is the natural wood, which also contains a
variety of tannins and sugars, and flavors such as
vanilla. Despite the name, 'green' whiskey is not
green. It is as clear as vodka. All of whiskey's color
comes from the wood.

Why white oak? In America, white oak is plentiful
and suitable because it is dense enough that the
barrels don't leak, but not so dense that the whiskey
can't penetrate and pick up the wood sugars and other
flavors. The federal rules require oak, though not white
oak specifically.

Traditionally, American whiskey is aged in
rackhouses. (They are also called rickhouses, barrel-
houses or simply warehouses.) These buildings, which
look like oversize barns, consist of a continuous,
interlocking web of wooden racks (or 'ricks') onto
which the barrels are rolled, so they rest horizontally
supported at either end. The rack structure that holds

the barrels is also the primary structure of the building, which is typically clad in sheets of corrugated steel. Rackhouses have many windows to promote air circulation. Warm temperatures cause the whiskey in the barrel to expand, forcing it deep into the wood. When it cools and contracts it infuses the rest of the whiskey with flavor and color from the wood. Meanwhile, the carbon in the char transforms and softens the fusel oils that make green whiskey taste so harsh. This in-and-out process—called the aging cycle—is repeated many times until the whiskey achieves its desired characteristics. Contact with air, oxygen in particular, is another important factor in favorably transforming the congeners.

All these and other factors—temperature, air circulation, humidity—can vary from location to location. This is why something that is true of people is also true of whiskey: age alone is no assurance of maturity. Whiskies aged in cool climates—let's say, for example, Scotland—take a long time to mature. During the long, cold Scottish winter the whiskey is essentially dormant. It isn't expanding and contracting, it isn't doing anything. In the warmer climate of Kentucky and Tennessee, the aging cycle is repeated more often and the whiskey matures more quickly. In fairness to the Scots, there is more to it than that. They make a style of whiskey that benefits most from long aging in used barrels. We make a style of whiskey than benefits most from shorter aging in new barrels. *Vive la différence.*

Even in the American Mid-South, some barrels cycle more often than others. This is because greater temperature extremes are inevitable in those sections of the rackhouse nearest to the exterior walls, especially near the top. Barrels near the exterior walls and near the top of the rackhouse age quickly. Barrels on the lower floors, especially in the center of the building, age slowly. One of the traditional ways to correct this imbalance is barrel rotation. This involves regularly changing the location of barrels in the rackhouse so they all mature at about the same rate. Rotation was necessary in the days when whiskey was shipped to customers in the barrel. A barrel might be topped off before it was shipped, to replace whatever volume had been lost through evaporation, but otherwise the barrel was shipped just as it came from the racks. Therefore, rotation was essential if you wanted a consistent product.

Today, this costly, labor-intensive practice is unnecessary and rarely done because all barrels are dumped for bottling, so any differences in the whiskey can be corrected in the dump tank. In preparation for a bottling run, a distiller will select barrels from different parts of the rackhouse, dump them all into a big tank (holding anywhere from 1,000 to 14,000 gallons) and taste the result. If it doesn't quite match the previous run of that product (they have rooms full of bottles holding reference samples), they go back and add some of whatever seems to be missing (older whiskey, younger whiskey, etc.). Another solution to the problem of uneven aging is to use low, single-story aging facilities in which maturation is naturally more uniform. The Four Roses rackhouses (sometimes called flathouses) at Lotus, near Bardstown, use this method. Some modern rackhouses have elaborate ventilation and heating systems to prevent dormancy during cold weather, and maximize air circulation all year.

In the countries that buy used bourbon barrels, the first refill is usually with base whiskey, which typically is high proof with little residual flavor, so it benefits from any bourbon flavor it can take from the wood. After the barrel is 'de-bourbonized' by this first refill, it can be used to age flavoring whiskies or single malts.

As already mentioned, another phenomenon that occurs when whiskey ages in wood is evaporation. A barrel of aging whiskey will lose about 4 percent of its volume per year, so that after 10 years a barrel may be barely half full. This is euphemistically called 'the angels' share' and it occurs everywhere spirits are aged in wood. (The attribution of it to angels probably originated in the Cognac region of France.) Peculiarly, however, in some environs the angels take more water and in others they take more alcohol, so the proof of the spirit in the barrel may go up, down, or stay about the same. The reason for this has to do with the interaction of alcohol molecules and water molecules with the wood, each other, and the atmosphere. A more scientific explanation than that you won't get from me. In Scotland, especially in rackhouses close to the sea, the proof tends to go down. In the American Mid-South, especially in the hottest parts of the rackhouses (typically the top), the proof tends to go up. This is why a recent edition of 15-year-old, barrel proof George T. Stagg bourbon is an eye-popping 142.7 proof.

A tip: Do not try to carry a bottle of Stagg bourbon onto an airplane. The Transportation Safety Administration (TSA) considers anything over 140 proof to be a hazardous material.

Another tip: all macho posturing aside, the TSA is right. Drinking 142.7 proof whiskey straight generally is not a good idea. This is the case for several reasons. First, that much pure alcohol quickly numbs your taste and smell receptors. The point of drinking a fine whiskey is to taste it, not simply to 'dose' yourself with alcohol. That is the second reason not to drink at high proof. Even people not predisposed to alcoholism can get into trouble when drinking alcohol at very high proofs. It quickly becomes difficult to accurately monitor and manage how much alcohol you are introducing into your system, something of which you should always be aware. Third, extremely high proof spirits can have a corrosive effect on your esophagus, stomach, etc.

So why do they sell whiskey at proofs in excess of 100? Premium whiskey is bottled at high proof to give you, the consumer, the ability to dilute it for drinking purposes according to your personal preference. It also means you are paying for whiskey, not water, which makes it a better value. A tiny sip of high proof spirit, just to experience it, won't hurt you but you generally should not drink any spirit above 100 proof without diluting it first with some room temperature water. A formula for accurately diluting a spirit to the desired proof is included in a later chapter.

Getting back to the wood, there are two primary companies that make barrels for the American whiskey industry. Bluegrass Cooperage, owned by Brown-Forman, is in Louisville. Bluegrass supplies the three Brown-Forman distilleries as well as other companies. Independent Stave, founded in 1912, has barrel plants in Lebanon, Missouri, and Lebanon,

Kentucky. You can distinguish between the Independent Stave barrels made in Kentucky and the ones made in Missouri by looking at the rivets used to hold the steel hoops together. The Kentucky barrels have a 'K' on the rivet heads and the Missouri barrels have a 'M.' Recently some smaller cooperages have begun to break into the whiskey barrel business.

The white oak used for American whiskey barrels comes primarily from the Ozark Mountains of Arkansas and Missouri, from trees that are 40 to 100 years old. It first goes to stave mills near the forests, where it is roughly cut. Then it is shipped to the cooperages, where it is either air- or kiln-dried, according to the distiller's specifications. Then the staves are planed and shaped. Barrel heads also are roughly cut at the mill and finished at the cooperage.

Although barrels in various stages of completion move around a modern cooperage on motorized conveyors, assembly is still done by hand. It takes a skilled craftsman to vary stave sizes and quickly form a barrel so that it will not leak. A perfect fit is crucial because no adhesives or nails are ever used. All that holds a barrel together are its six steel hoops. Barrel staves are slightly fuller in the middle than they are at the ends. The assembler arranges them loosely in a framework that approximates the location of the two lowest hoops. Then the barrels go through a steam bath to soften the wood. After the steam, a steel cable noose is used to pull the other end together. Additional temporary hoops are added to that end of the barrel and the noose is released. The tension caused by the bowed staves straining against the hoops is what holds the barrel together.

After all of the temporary hoops are in place, the barrel—still open at both ends—is conveyed to the charring furnace. Just as customers specify air- or kiln-drying, they also specify how deeply they want their barrels charred. Seven depths are available and are a function of how long the gas-fueled charring jets are allowed to burn. The heaviest char takes about a minute. Char ratings, from the lightest to the heaviest, are 1, 1.5, 2, 2.5, 3, 3.5 and 4. The heaviest or #4 char is considered to be the physical limit of the wood. Any deeper and the barrel is supposed to lose physical integrity and collapse, but in reality chars up to #7 have been done successfully. Most American whiskey distillers use a #3 char.

After charring, the temporary hoops are replaced by permanent ones, the heads are added and the bung hole is drilled. The bung hole must be placed in the center of a stave cut wide enough to accommodate it. This is called the bung stave. The fully-assembled barrels are trucked to the distillery where they are filled by inserting a nozzle into the bung hole. After the barrel is pumped full, the hole is plugged with a wooden bung, usually made of poplar, which is pounded in tightly with a large mallet. Aging whiskey is regularly checked. Traditionally, this meant removing the bung and inserting a 'whiskey thief,' which is a grand name for a cup attached to a long stick. This process was time-consuming, and tended to degrade the bung and cause leakage around the bung hole. Today, a cordless electric drill is used to poke a tiny hole in the side of the barrel. Whiskey immediately shoots out in a thin stream and is captured in a waiting bottle (and never, ever, in the warehouseman's waiting mouth). A small wooden peg is then used to plug the hole. The date and serial number of the barrel are written on the bottle, which goes to the lab for testing.

'Testing,' it should be noted, does involve some use of scientific instruments, but mostly it is a euphemism for drinking. The tried-and-true method of analyzing whiskey is to look at it, smell it and drink it. The master distiller does this, but every distillery also has a tasting panel of several experienced hands who are given this awesome responsibility.

Because American straights are aged exclusively in new charred barrels, no other spirit owes more to its time in wood. Happily for the preservation of the ancient craft of cooperage, this is the only way to make an American straight whiskey. The barrel is as much an 'ingredient' of bourbon, rye and Tennessee whiskey as are the grains, water and yeast. You can make liquor, you can even make whiskey, without new, charred oak barrels, but you can't make bourbon, rye or Tennessee whiskey.

Chapter Five

The Last Step: Selling Bourbon in Bottles.

One of the last major changes to the way bourbon is made and sold was bottling, a practice so ubiquitous now that we don't even think about it. But bottled bourbon was rare before 1870, didn't become common until after 1903, and didn't become universal until Prohibition.

Until the end of the 19th century, whiskey was almost always transported in barrels. Sometimes it was the same barrel in which it had been aged. Even more common was the practice of wholesale whiskey merchants, who would buy bulk whiskey from distillers and create proprietary brands by mixing together whiskies from several sources. They would then re-barrel the results and ship them to their customers. Although some distillers sold directly to saloons, general stores, and even consumers in their immediate neighborhood, more distant sales were the province of wholesalers. Some well-heeled whiskey drinkers could afford to buy their household bourbon supply in barrel lots, from wholesalers and even directly from distillers, but most could not. The more typical distribution chain was for a distiller to sell his whiskey to a wholesaler who would sell it, also by the barrel, to a retailer such as a saloon or general store. If the whiskey was aged before sale, the aging probably was done by the wholesaler, not the distiller.

In some cases, wholesalers rectified the whiskey they bought. 'To rectify' literally means 'to fix,' and that is what rectifiers felt they were doing. They 'fixed' the whiskey either by redistilling it, or by filtering it through large stands of charcoal, as is still the practice in Tennessee. They would then combine rectified whiskey with some good aged whiskey and maybe also add fruit juices or other substances to give the liquor body, flavor and color. Large wholesalers sold a variety of products ranging from vile concoctions that contained little or no aged whiskey to mixtures of good, aged bourbon. The true aged whiskies were the more desirable products and, consequently, more expensive but there were no truth in labeling laws then, so misrepresentation was common.

At the saloon or general store level, the proprietor would tap the barrel by inserting a spigot into the barrel head. A bartender might then transfer some of the whiskey into bottles for ease of serving. Bar patrons could purchase whiskey by-the-drink or by-the-bottle, but they were buying only the whiskey. The bottles were always reused. Fancy saloons had beautiful blown glass decanters, provided by the whiskey makers, with the whiskey brand names etched or embossed on their sides. For carry-out, customers brought their own bottle, jug or other container to be filled from the barrel.

This was the universal practice prior to the 20th century because glass bottles were individually handmade and expensive. Selling whiskey in bottles would have been ridiculous, because the bottle would have cost more than the whiskey inside it. (On second thought, maybe that is not so ridiculous, since it probably describes most premium vodkas.)

Unfortunately, this distribution system made it easy for wholesalers to cheat their retail customers and for retailers to cheat consumers. Wholesale whiskey in those days was sold by 'drummers,' traveling salesmen who carried bottled samples of the products their employer had available for sale. The drummer would provide the prospective shopkeeper or saloon owner with a taste from his sample bottle and, on that basis, an order for one or more barrels would be placed.

This was the first point at which larceny might occur. The barrels that were eventually delivered to the customer might or might not contain the same product that was in the drummer's sample bottle. Some wholesalers were more trustworthy in this respect than others. Likewise, a barrel of whiskey in a saloon or general store often did not contain what the proprietor and even the name burned into the barrelhead said it did. Unscrupulous retailers would commonly water their whiskey or extend it with green whiskey or neutral spirits, maybe some lanolin to give it body, prune juice for color and flavor, and acid to create that burning sensation in the throat. These are some of the less disgusting practices. Even if all a retailer did was pour cheaper whiskey into a better brand's barrel, you still weren't getting what you paid for.

In 1870, Old Forester became the first bourbon to be shipped and sold exclusively in bottles. It was the brainchild of George Garvin Brown, the founder of Brown-Forman. George Brown was a whiskey merchant—a wholesaler—based in Louisville. His grandfather, William, had been an early Kentucky settler and farmer but probably not a distiller. George got into the business of selling whiskey with his older half-brother, John Thompson Street Brown.

George Brown decided to create a product that would be sold exclusively in bottles because he intended to market it to physicians. Doctors in those days widely prescribed whiskey as a remedy for many ailments. Brown had heard many doctors complain about the irregular quality of the whiskey their patients could obtain, due to the practices already described. If this was a problem in Louisville, so close to the whiskey's source, he knew it had to be an even bigger problem in more distant markets. So Brown decided to create a product doctors everywhere could prescribe with confidence. If a whiskey was available only in sealed bottles, he reasoned, the purchaser could be confident about its source and, therefore, about its contents. To reinforce this message, Brown put a handwritten and signed pledge to that effect on his product's label.

Brown's Old Forester whiskey was indeed reliable, but expensive, and the idea of bottled bourbon did not catch on with the general public until the 1890s, but

Brown had been the first and his company, Brown-Forman, had gained a reputation for quality and integrity in the process. That reputation was especially valuable in the rapidly growing markets west of the Mississippi, where the abuses of the old system had been the most egregious.

Two changes that made bottled whiskey more common were passage of the Bottled-In-Bond Act in 1897, and the invention of the first economical automatic bottle-making machine in 1903. The Bottled-In-Bond Act made the federal government the guarantor of whiskey authenticity, but only if the whiskey was sold in sealed bottles. The automatic bottle-making machine made bottles much more affordable. The final step occurred during Prohibition and continued after repeal. During Prohibition, whiskey could be legally sold only by the very few companies who had been granted licenses to hold and bottle whiskey for medicinal use. Those licenses required them to sell the whiskey to pharmacists only in sealed one-pint bottles. After Prohibition, though a wider variety of sizes was authorized, whiskey could be sold only in bottles.

Today, it is illegal to sell whiskey in barrels, or in any container larger than 1.75 liters, to anyone other than a licensed distiller or bottler. Several distilleries—including Brown-Forman's Jack Daniel's—will sell you a barrel of their whiskey, and even let you come to the distillery to pick it out, but you have to let them bottle it for you. You can, however, then have the empty barrel as a souvenir. Presumably, if you decided to take the barrel home and empty all of the whiskey back into it, no one would try to stop you.

Chapter Six

Haydens, Wathens and Old Grand-Dad.

In 1987, the Jim Beam Brands Company acquired National Distillers. Beam immediately closed the two Kentucky distilleries where National had made bourbon. Beam already had two whiskey distilleries of its own in Kentucky, at Clermont and Boston, with enough production capacity to supply the combined portfolio. Besides, there was a glut of whiskey at the time. Beam wanted National for the rest of its portfolio, not for its bourbons.

National's flagship bourbon had been Old Grand-Dad. There was irony in the fact that Old Grand-Dad would now be made at Jim Beam. The Clermont distillery sits only a few miles from the site of the original Old Grand-Dad plant at Hobbs Station. After spending time in Louisville, Frankfort and even Canada, Old Grand-Dad was back where it started.

Both the Clermont and Hobbs Station sites were chosen for their railroad access. After railroads came to that part of Kentucky in the 1860s, the only sensible place to build a distillery was along their tracks. Whiskey was shipped in barrels and with a full barrel of whiskey weighing about 500 pounds, proximity to a railroad line made distribution much easier. Many current and past distilleries in the Bardstown area are located along that same branch of the Louisville and Nashville Railroad. Only the 'My Old Kentucky Dinner Train' uses those tracks today, for excursion trips. All of the whiskey is shipped by truck.

The original Old Grand-Dad Distillery was built by R. B. Hayden and F. L. Ferriell in 1882. Raymond Hayden had been a distiller all his life, like his father and grandfather before him. Basil Hayden, Raymond's grandfather, came to Kentucky from Maryland in 1796, settling in the countryside outside of Bardstown. He was a typical farmer-distiller, making whiskey for his family's use, selling some to his neighbors, and shipping the rest down the river to New Orleans. He was succeeded in this enterprise by his son, Lewis, and his grandson, Raymond. Raymond's mother, Polly, also came from an old and distinguished Kentucky whiskey-making family, the Dants.

As the region became more developed, whiskey distilling became more commercialized. With Kentucky whiskey being shipped all over the country on the new railroads, distillers who wanted to sell their whiskey directly to customers and not through middlemen needed to develop strong brand identities. When Hayden and Ferriell built their new distillery they decided to call their bourbon 'Old Grand-Dad' in honor of Raymond's grandfather. They also made a straight rye whiskey. Ferriell, the junior partner in the new distillery, was 37 when he went into business with Hayden, who was 61. Ferriell had fought for the Union in the Civil War and after the conflict had worked for three years as a 'government man,' that is, a collector of the federal excise tax on distilled spirits. The Hobbs Station plant had access to two springs. The distillery had a mashing capacity of 100 bushels of grain per day. The rackhouses had a storage capacity of 7,000 barrels.

Raymond Hayden never married and had no children. When he died in 1885, Philetus S. Barber, a wealthy Nelson County furrier and stock breeder, purchased controlling interest in the firm from Hayden's estate. The company was renamed Barber, Ferriell & Co. Barber died in 1894 and was succeeded by his son-in-law, Lou Baldwin. In 1899, Baldwin and Ferriell sold out to the three Wathen brothers, John Bernard (J.B.) Richard Nicholas (Nick), and Martin Athanasius (Nace). Through all of these ownership and company name changes, the name of the company's principal product, Old Grand-Dad bourbon, did not change.

In 1899, when they bought the Hobbs Station distillery and its brand, the Wathen brothers were on a roll. Their immigrant ancestor, John Wathen, had come from England in 1645 to be part of Lord Baltimore's Maryland colony where Roman Catholics, in flight from persecution by the then-ascendant Puritans, could worship freely. Their grandfather, Henry Hudson Wathen, came to Kentucky from Maryland in 1787 and settled in what is now Marion County. The Wathens, like the Haydens, were among the first Roman Catholic settlers in Kentucky. It is commonly assumed that most early whiskey makers were Scots or Scots-Irish, but they were also Irish like Henry McKenna, German like Jacob Beam (originally Boehm), and English like Henry Wathen.

Like most of his neighbors, Henry Wathen was a farmer-distiller, as was his son, Richard, who became prosperous as a farmer and made whiskey as a sideline. In 1863, as the Civil War raged, Richard's eldest son, John Bernard (J.B.), age 19, dropped out of college to come home and run the family distillery. The War Between the States was generally good for Kentucky's distillers, many of whom sympathized with the Confederacy. Jim Beam, born in 1864, was given the middle name of Beauregard after the popular Confederate general who captured Fort Sumter. William Weller's sons fought for the South and the Samuels family had close links to Quantrill's Raiders. Since Kentucky was officially neutral in the conflict, the distillers were able to sell their whiskey to customers on both sides. It was during the war that whiskey-making in Kentucky evolved into a truly commercial enterprise. We don't know for sure why J. B. Wathen quit school to take over his family's distillery, but it may have been to take advantage of a booming business opportunity.

Whiskey sales continued to boom after the war. By 1871, J. B. Wathen had built what had been a minor part of his father's farm into a large and successful business. That year, for some unnamed health reason, J. B. suddenly closed the family distillery. Four years later, with his health restored, J. B. and his younger brother, Nick, bought a bigger and more modern distillery closer to Lebanon, the county seat. Their youngest brother, Nace, would join them a few years later. In 1880, the three Wathen brothers built another even larger distillery in Louisville, at Broadway and 26th Street. They continued to grow and prosper. In 1899, they bought the Old Grand-Dad Distillery and made Nace its president. Although it came late in the careers of the original Wathen brothers, Old Grand-Dad bourbon was destined to be the Wathen family's best known and most successful brand.

J. B. was the leader of the Wathen clan. He was a highly successful and respected businessman, with a distilling career that spanned nearly 50 years. In 1867 he had married Margaret Adams, granddaughter of a nephew of the second president. Their sons Richard Eugene (Dick), John Bernard Jr., and Otho Hill were educated at Georgetown and Notre Dame before returning to take their places in the family whiskey business. There was in Kentucky at that time a 'bourbon aristocracy' and the Wathens were a big part of it.

Then came National Prohibition. The original Wathen brothers were all dead by then, with Nace having died in 1912, and J. B. and Nick both passing in 1919, shortly before Prohibition took effect. Whatever family business was going to continue would now be up to the next generation.

During Prohibition, one of the biggest enforcement problems was what to do with all the whiskey that was still aging in the nation's rackhouses. Although the government could legally prevent it from being sold for consumption, they couldn't legally confiscate it and no provisions had been made for the government to purchase it from its owners so it could be destroyed. Instead, rackhouses with aging whiskey in them were simply locked up. The rackhouses and their contents were still private property, but the owners weren't allowed access to them without government permission. With hundreds of these rackhouses scattered across Kentucky and other states, many in remote rural areas, it was impossible for enforcement officials to guard them all, and with prospects for the owners ever being able to profit from their property legally looking increasingly dim, pilfering became rampant. Undoubtedly, many of the thieves had cooperation from the whiskey's owners, who could make at least a little cash by stealing their own whiskey and selling it illegally. It probably was going to be stolen at any event.

In the above-ground market, the only way whiskey could be sold was for medical purposes. To stop illegal diversion and ensure the availability of whiskey for medicinal use, the government eventually took steps to protect whiskey stocks. It ordered all remaining whiskey to be consolidated into a handful of large rackhouses, licensed for that purpose and located mostly in urban areas where they could be guarded more easily. Although the original owner of the whiskey could pay the consolidation warehouse a fee for storage, it was more typical to simply sell the barrels to the consolidator for whatever they would bring, along with all rights to the brand names that went with them. Even if the distiller expected Prohibition eventually to be repealed, most of them were so strapped financially that they had to sell.

The three sons of J. B. Wathen went into this business with gusto, consolidating all of their family's remaining operations in Louisville. They renamed the firm the American Medicinal Spirits Company (AMS) and it became the largest consolidation warehouse and medicinal whiskey operation in Kentucky. In addition to Old Grand-Dad and other Wathen family brands, AMS acquired the Old Crow, Hill & Hill, Bourbon DeLuxe and Hermitage labels.

During Prohibition, people who wanted a drink could usually find one. As the humorist Will Rogers once quipped, "Prohibition is better than no liquor at all." In big cities like Chicago, illegal breweries and distilleries operated under the protection of criminal gangs, and corrupt local governments and police forces looked the other way. In Chicago's Little Italy neighborhood there were dozens of small basement distilleries in private homes, making a sort of crude brandy. Sam Giancana, eventual boss of the Chicago Outfit, started his criminal career collecting the output of these small distilleries for central distribution. Meanwhile, whiskey from Scotland was being smuggled in all along the East Coast and Canadian whiskey was being smuggled in across that lengthy border. AMS had its own Canadian outpost. They recruited Guy Beam as their distiller and produced bourbon-style whiskey to be sold under two of their most prominent brand names, Old Crow and Old Grand-Dad.

In 1924, Seton Potter reorganized the insolvent Distillers' Securities Corporation (an outgrowth of the nefarious Whiskey Trust of the 1880s and 90s) as the National Distillers Products Corporation, to produce

industrial alcohol, medicinal alcohol and yeast. He
began buying up consolidation warehouses and their
contents. By 1927, National was the largest share-
holder in AMS. In 1929, the Wathens sold the rest of
their company to National and the eldest brother, Dick,
became an executive there.

After Prohibition, the old Wathen family distillery
in Lebanon was returned to production by a cousin,
John A. Wathen. It subsequently was sold to Schenley,
the other big U.S. company besides National in the
post-Prohibition spirits industry. Another cousin, Nick
Wathen's daughter, Florence Ellen, married Tom
Medley. The Medleys were a Western Kentucky family
who operated several distilleries in and around
Owensboro. Two of Tom and Florence's children, Ben
Medley and Wathen Medley, became prominent in the
post-Prohibition whiskey business. Another member of
that clan, Charles Medley, was the family's last active
distiller. He made bourbon for Glenmore until that
company was sold to United Distillers, which closed
Charlie's Owensboro plant in 1993. Today, he and his
son sell a small batch bourbon called Wathen's.

The original Old Grand-Dad Distillery did not
reopen after Prohibition. Only the plant's concrete
footers and a crumbling creek rock wall around the
old spring remain at the Hobbs Station site. In 1940,
National Distillers bought the K. Taylor Distilling Co. at
Elkhorn Forks on the Georgetown Pike, just outside of
Frankfort, and gave it the Old Grand-Dad name. This
distillery is in a beautiful location where the two
branches of Elkhorn Creek come together, amidst
sparkling cascades, rocky bluffs and thick woods even
today. The first distillery at Elkhorn Forks (also called

Forks of the Elkhorn) was built in 1869 by W. J. Baker. One of his brands had a large swastika on its label, long before Germany's National Socialists appropriated and debased that ancient symbol. In 1901, Baker and other members of his family were part of a group led by John D. Hinde and his son, Thomas, that erected a new and larger distillery on the site and called it the Frankfort Distillery. They stopped operations there in 1916. During Prohibition, this plant also was a consolidation warehouse, like AMS in Louisville. On July 21, 1924, a fire of unknown origin destroyed one of the rackhouses and, with it, 1,500 barrels and 2,156 cases of whiskey. By 1928, all of the whiskey was gone and the facility fell into disrepair. Tom Hinde and his associates sold the property and, after Prohibition, built a new distillery in Louisville which they gave the Frankfort name, although it was better known by the name of its principal brand, Four Roses.

In 1933, the Elkhorn Forks property was acquired by associates of Kenner Taylor, one of the sons of E. H. Taylor (founder of Old Taylor). Kenner Taylor died shortly before the new distillery opened in 1937, but it was called the K. Taylor Distilling Co. anyway. National bought it a few years later and made its first entry of 112 barrels of Old Grand-Dad there on November 26, 1940. Old Grand-Dad continued to be made at Elkhorn Forks until Jim Beam Brands bought National in 1987. Whiskey is stored and bottled there today, but Jim Beam has never fired up the stills. Old Grand-Dad is now distilled by Beam at either Clermont or Boston.

Of the many bourbons once made and sold by the Wathen family, Old Grand-Dad is the most prominent one still sold today. One of the bourbons in Jim Beam's

Small Batch Collection is named in honor of the original Old Grand-Dad, Basil Hayden. The story of American whiskey is a story of families and at least six of those families (the Beams, Dants, Haydens, Medleys, Taylors and Wathens) have touched the story of Old Grand-Dad, making it one of the richest in bourbon country.

Chapter Seven

The Elusive Bourbon Renaissance.

Bourbon consumption in the U.S. has declined every year since 1978 and for almost that long, bourbon marketers have been predicting a revival. Is it finally here? Or is recent heightened interest in bourbon whiskey just the last gasp of a drink on its way to oblivion, barely kept alive as a novelty like mead or applejack? For this chapter only, the term 'bourbon' will be synonymous with 'American whiskey' and encompass category leader Jack Daniel's Tennessee Whisky, other non-bourbon straights such as rye, and American blended whiskey.

Once upon a time in America, if you wanted to drink a distilled spirit, bourbon was just about your only option. Rum, popular during the colonial period, fell out of favor during the Revolution for being too British. Then came applejack, the distilled form of hard cider, but as a crop to grow, cereal grains were better than apples, so soon whiskey was the main drink. That it was almost all *American* whiskey goes without saying. Only the very rich drank anything imported.

That all changed with Prohibition. People drank whatever they could get and often that was scotch or Canadian whiskey, or cocktails made with neutral spirits. You could only get real American straight whiskey with a doctor's prescription.

When Prohibition ended, the American distilling industry tried to get back on its feet, but it wasn't easy. Except for a handful of distilleries that had medicinal whiskey licenses, most plants had been picked apart for anything of value. In particular, anything that contained copper had been stripped and sold, which meant most of the critical distilling equipment was gone. Although National Prohibition went into effect in January of 1920, it had been coming for decades. Many states had already gone dry when a national wartime suspension of distilling activity was imposed in 1917. This meant that America's distilleries had not operated in anything like a normal fashion for twenty years or more, so even the few intact plants were technologically obsolete. The industry needed to rebuild from scratch. It did, and by the end of the 1930s it was ready to move forward.

Then, even more suddenly than the blow of Prohibition, disaster struck again in the form of the Japanese bombing of Pearl Harbor and the beginning of America's involvement in World War II. Distilleries were ordered to produce alcohol for military use. Prohibition was over and whiskey was legal again, but it remained in short supply during the war years.

After the war it took a few years again to rebuild aged whiskey stocks but then bourbon consumption took off, growing steadily for more than 30 years. Then it began a 20 year nose-dive. Americans today drink only about half as much bourbon as they did 30 years ago. Some people explain this fact by observing that Americans are simply drinking less, but not really. Not *that much* less. Overall consumption of alcoholic beverages has declined but only slightly in the last three decades, especially compared to bourbon's steep crash.

For such a dramatic and sustained loss to occur, two things had to happen. First, large numbers of people had to *stop* drinking bourbon and, second, even larger numbers of young people had to *not start* drinking it when they reached legal age. Both of these things happened to bourbon. Most observers attribute bourbon's long decline to the wider availability of alternative intoxicants, both legal and illegal, that began during the 1960s, along with the spirit of experimentation and discovery that encouraged people to try anything new. Affluence was another factor because people had enough money to try more costly imported products. The growing acceptability of public drinking by women was significant because they did not have established drinking habits (or macho prejudices) and gravitated toward drinks that tasted good, which tended to be made from neutral or nearly-neutral spirits like vodka and white rum mixed with soft drinks or fruit juices.

Regardless of the reasons, bourbon sales plummeted beginning in the 1970s and as they plunged, industry leaders kept predicting the advent of a new 'bourbon boom,' even as the smartest of them rapidly diversified their product portfolios. The logic for the coming bourbon boom was simple. Just as the sixties generation had rejected the drinks of its parents, so the next generation would reject the drinks of its baby-boomer parents and turn back to bourbon. Some even believed the baby boomers themselves would rediscover bourbon as they aged and became more conservative. Occasional bursts of patriotism, such as the one we are experiencing now, also were supposed to spark renewed interest in the 'All-American Spirit.' So has run the wishful thinking of many industry pundits.

Even some practical, cynical analysts predicted an eventual bourbon revival. They simply concluded that the industry must eventually hit bottom and reach its natural level in the larger universe of adult beverage products. At that point, the bourbon segment could start to compete for incremental share gains and slowly rebuild volume and profitability. That, essentially, is what has occurred in the last decade or so, at least in terms of profitability if not overall volume.

For bourbon marketers, projecting sales long term is more than an academic exercise. Because of whiskey's long aging cycle, a company must produce today the amount of bourbon it will be able to sell four or more years from now. If they guess wrong and make either too little or too much, they lose money. Bourbon only gets better in wood up to a point, so distillers can't necessarily recover the cost of additional, unplanned aging. The prudent distiller wants to make enough but not too much, because oversupply will depress profits. The guess has to be almost exactly right.

So if there is a bourbon revival going on and if it is going to keep growing and peak sometime in the next six or seven years, it is important to know about it now. Unfortunately, if there is a major revival coming, it hasn't shown up in the numbers yet. For the last decade or so, ever since the tumble ended, total U.S. bourbon sales have been essentially flat. The only good news bourbon makers have had in the last decade or so has been the growth of exports and the growth of super-premium or luxury bottlings, first internationally and then domestically. Both of these trends, while making only a modest impact on overall volume, have been terrific for profitability. The other good news for bourbon-makers is that industry consolidation has more-or-less stabilized. Every player now is a big, diversified company. No one makes just bourbon. Jim Beam is the largest bourbon producer but its parent, Fortune Brands, makes everything from faucets to golf balls.

A glance at bourbon production tables reveals another happy trend. After steadily drawing down overstocked inventories for roughly 20 years, the production curve finally stabilized about fifteen years ago. Companies can now keep their depletions just about even with their production. Whiskey in storage peaked in 1971 at more than 950 million gallons. There is about half that much in aging warehouses today, a little bit more than a four year supply at current sales levels.

Every year, the traditional bourbon drinker gets a year older. Every year, a few more of them die. New bourbon drinkers are not stepping up to the bar in sufficient numbers to take all of their places. The single

malt scotch and imported vodka booms have been real
and sustained. The long-anticipated bourbon boom is
still mostly vapor. This is not to say the industry is
bleak, just the opposite. Overall sales are flat because
the growth in super-premiums is offset by the
continuing decline of the standard product, so
profitability keeps improving. The industry is now
stable and all of the companies still in bourbon have
figured out how to make money at it. Times are pretty
good.

What we are not seeing, however, is any new
companies entering the fray. Part of the problem is the
way the industry grew back after the repeal of
Prohibition. The regulatory scheme put in place in
1933 favors big, concentrated, well-financed producers who can pay their taxes on time, keep all the
records the government demands, and who have too
much at stake to risk it by getting out of line. Those
kinds of companies—big multinationals for the most
part—favor big, highly automated distilleries. Despite
the hype of some marketers, there are no little country
distilleries. The smallest fill about 40,000 barrels a
year. The largest fill 100,000 or more barrels a year.
Despite the bright forecast for premium bourbons, the
cost of entry for new producers is simply too high.

The problem with this situation is that it is hard to
develop an enthusiast community like there is for
wine, craft beer, or single malt scotch when you have
so few producers. If you want to, you probably can
taste something from every bourbon producer in a
single sitting. There are a couple of small craft
distilleries in the United States, but they mostly make
clear fruit spirits in the *eau de vie* style, which don't

have to be aged. Generally, these small distillers don't make whiskey. Some distillers, in particular Buffalo Trace and Heaven Hill, have done a good job of searching their rackhouses for whiskey that, for some reason or another, has developed an unusual or original taste, which allows them to release a plethora of brands and expressions with real differences among them, including some that are truly original such as Buffalo Trace's George T. Stagg.

Brown-Forman's decision almost ten years ago to restore the Woodford Reserve Distillery and reopen it as a small producer using pot stills was a hopeful sign, but that hope has been tempered by their reluctance to release any of that plant's output, except mixed with column-distilled whiskey from Louisville in its namesake Woodford Reserve bourbon. Corporate culture may be getting in the way here. Brown-Forman's business model has always been to be one of the top producers in any category in which they participate. If they can't lead in a category, they get out. Releasing limited appeal, niche products is contrary to that philosophy. Brown-Forman has, however, put a toe into this niche with the introduction of Old Forester Birthday Bourbon in 2002, a limited edition release that will offer new expressions annually.

Initiatives that give master distillers the freedom to select more imaginatively and create brands suited for more adventurous palates are one way to keep bourbon interesting. It is also important to educate consumers and go beyond empty clichés in describing these new products. This is what it will take to keep bourbon fresh, interesting and challenging long-term, both for enthusiasts and for the general public. Ultimately, it would be great if a craft distilling movement would come into being for American whiskey, but if it is on its way it is only just beginning and is many years away from maturity. Without variety and vitality continuously coming from all of these sources, bourbon—which is now often touted as the 'old-new' drink—will become 'old-old' again very quickly.

Chapter Eight

An American Whiskey Sampling Guide.

The purpose of this chapter is to help you sample the output of every American whiskey distillery. Such a guide is necessary because most distilleries sell essentially the same whiskey under multiple brand names, so if you buy bourbons at random you might wind up tasting the same whiskey over and over, and miss others. I will suggest a couple of each distillery's products for sampling. Where possible, I have tried to recommend both a higher-priced and a lower-priced product from each distillery. I also will take this opportunity to name each distillery's parent company.

With some caveats, there are 14 active whiskey distilleries in the United States today. Here is the list, the caveats follow.

The list:
1. Jim Beam–Clermont, KY
2. Jim Beam–Boston, KY

3. Barton–Bardstown, KY
4. Maker's Mark–Loretto, KY
5. Heaven Hill–Louisville, KY
6. Four Roses–Lawrenceburg, KY
7. Wild Turkey–Lawrenceburg, KY
8. Jack Daniel's–Lynchburg, TN
9. George Dickel–Tullahoma, TN
10. A. Smith Bowman–Fredericksburg, VA
11. Early Times–Shively, KY
12. Woodford Reserve–Versailles, KY
13. Buffalo Trace–Frankfort, KY
14. Anchor Distilling–San Francisco, CA

The caveats:

- A. Smith Bowman has a small pot still which it uses to redistill whiskey supplied by Buffalo Trace. Because their Virginia Gentleman bourbon, which continues to be a well known and widely distributed brand, originates from that still they are on the list. They are now owned by Buffalo Trace, which says it will continue the Virginia operation.

- McCormick is a small distillery in Missouri that has made whiskey in the past, may still have that capability, and may actually make some from time to time. They sell American whiskey, but whether or not they actually made any of the whiskey they currently sell I have been unable to determine with certainty. They aren't on the list and based on the products by them that I have tasted, you aren't missing a thing if you never try them.

- Anchor Distilling is a very small distillery in San Francisco that makes a rye whiskey called Old Potrero. Although overall volume is very small, the product is widely distributed, so they are on the list.

- There are a couple of other small craft distilleries in the United States. At least two, St. George in Alameda, California, and Clear Creek in Portland, Oregon, have experimented with whiskey but their products are not widely distributed. They are not on the list.

Jim Beam. Jim Beam Brands Co. distills bourbon at two locations; Clermont and Boston, both in Kentucky and both near Bardstown. They have rackhouses at six or seven different locations around Bardstown and Frankfort. Beam makes two distinct bourbon formulas, Jim Beam and Old Grand-Dad, from which they produce a variety of different whiskies. They also make straight rye. They seem to use the two distilleries interchangeably, so it is not possible to say whether a certain product came from Boston or Clermont. Their parent company is Fortune Brands.

To taste the Jim Beam formula, skip the ubiquitous white label and try Jim Beam Black Label or Knob Creek. To taste the Old Grand-Dad formula, try Old Grand-Dad Bonded or 114. To taste their rye, try Old Overholt.

Barton. The Barton Distillery in Bardstown, Kentucky, stands on the site of several historic distilleries including its direct predecessor, Tom Moore. They make bourbon and rye. Barton's parent company is Constellation Brands.

Barton's excellent Very Old Barton bourbon is the best selling whiskey in Kentucky, but not widely available elsewhere. Their not-nearly-as-good Ten High is widely available. Their rye is the hard-to-find Fleischmann's.

Maker's Mark. The Maker's Mark Distillery in Loretto, Kentucky, has rackhouses at a couple of different locations, including at the old T. W. Samuels site near Bardstown. The Samuels family founded and still runs Maker's Mark, but the company is owned by Allied-Domecq.

Maker's Mark makes only one product, Maker's Mark bourbon, so that is the one to try. It is a wheat-flavored bourbon.

Heaven Hill. The Heaven Hill distillery is in Louisville, although the company's roots—along with its corporate offices, bottling house and most of its rackhouses—are in and around Bardstown. The distillery is on the site of the old Bernheim Distillery. A new distillery was built there in 1991 by United Distillers, then part of Guinness, which subsequently merged with Grand Metropolitan and became Diageo. Heaven Hill lost its original distillery in Bardstown to a fire in 1996. It bought the Bernheim facility from Diageo and resumed distilling there in 2000. In the interim, Heaven Hill bought whiskey from other distillers and also rented time at other distilleries to make its own whiskey formulas under master distiller Parker Beam's supervision. Whiskey sold by Heaven Hill today may come from any of those sources. Obviously their older whiskies, such as the Evan Williams single barrel and both of the Elijah Craig expressions, should be whiskey from the original Bardstown distillery. Heaven Hill is owned by the Shapira family.

Heaven Hill makes at least two bourbon formulas as well as a straight rye. To taste their rye-flavored bourbon, try one of the Evan Williams expressions, either the serviceable black label 7-year-old, or the better Single Barrel Vintage. To taste their wheat-flavored bourbon, try Old Fitzgerald, preferably the bottled-in-bond expression. For straight rye, try Rittenhouse, preferably the 100 proof bottled-in-bond.

Four Roses. The Four Roses Distillery in Lawrenceburg, Kentucky, has a long history dating back to a small distillery started nearby by 'Old Joe' Payton in 1818. It was acquired by Seagrams during World War II and renamed Four Roses. In 2001, the Four Roses brand and distillery were acquired by Kirin Brewery.

Four Roses is unusual in that it makes several different bourbon formulas—using different combinations of corn, rye and malt, and different yeasts—then mixes them together to achieve a particular taste profile, much like the way the Canadian blended whiskies for which Seagrams was best known are made. Their very drinkable standard Four Roses bourbon is primarily available in Kentucky and overseas, but wider U.S. distribution soon appears likely. Bulleit bourbon (made there but owned by Diageo) is a little more widely available but less characteristic of the distillery's style.

Wild Turkey. The Wild Turkey Distillery in Lawrenceburg, Kentucky, makes Wild Turkey bourbon, Wild Turkey rye and Wild Turkey liqueur. The distillery is in a beautiful location atop a deep gorge overlooking the Kentucky River. The heritage of this distillery is tied up with the Ripy family, once the most prominent distillers in Anderson County. They supplied whiskey for the Wild Turkey brand for years

until the brand's owners finally bought the distillery.
Wild Turkey is owned by Pernod-Ricard.

Although Wild Turkey bourbon is available in
several excellent expressions, you can't go wrong with
the standard 101 proof version. The 10-year-old
Russell's Reserve (named for master distiller Jimmy
Russell) is also excellent. Avoid the 80 proof version.
The rye, also 101 proof, is worth a taste as well.

Jack Daniel's. The Jack Daniel Distillery in
Lynchburg, Tennessee, is one of three American
whiskey distilleries owned by Brown-Forman. Headquartered in Louisville, Brown-Forman is a public
company but the founding Brown family still controls it.
In an industry where most distilleries have relocated
many times and changed ownership even more often,
Jack Daniel's is unusual in having had only two owners
in its long history, the Daniel-Motlow family, then
Brown-Forman.

The Lynchburg distillery makes several expressions of Jack Daniel's Tennessee whiskey. Try the
standard black label version. It is the most popular
American whiskey in the world, so they must be doing
something right.

George Dickel. The other distillery making
Tennessee whiskey is George Dickel in Tullahoma,
which is owned by Diageo. They were dark for about
four years during which time they drew down existing
inventory, so despite the long break, all of the whiskey
they sell was made at that plant. Try the No. 12
expression.

A. Smith Bowman. Founded just after Prohibition
on a farm that occupied much of what is now Reston,
Virginia, A. Smith Bowman's main brand has always

been Virginia Gentleman, which has won many bar bets for people whose friends insisted that bourbon could be made only in Kentucky. Today, as mentioned in the caveats, Virginia Gentleman performs a third distillation on whiskey double-distilled at Buffalo Trace, in Frankfort, which recently purchased A. Smith Bowman.

If you can find it, the 6-year-old, 90 proof version of Virginia Gentleman, nicknamed "the fox," is the one to try.

Early Times. The Early Times Distillery in Shively, Kentucky (a suburb of Louisville), makes two different formulas, Early Times Kentucky whiskey, technically not a bourbon because some of the whiskey is aged in used barrels, and Old Forester bourbon. The plant is owned by Brown-Forman. Whiskey distilled there from the Old Forester formula is also trucked to Brown-Forman's third American whiskey distillery, Woodford Reserve, where it is mixed with whiskey made there to create Woodford Reserve bourbon.

The 100 proof expression of Old Forester is the best product of this distillery to try.

Woodford Reserve. The distillery now known as Woodford Reserve (formerly Labrot & Graham), near Versailles, Kentucky, was founded in 1812 by Elijah Pepper and rose to prominence under his son, Oscar. Dr. James C. Crow was Oscar Pepper's distiller. Crow is credited with both the sour mash process and with being the first distiller to routinely and exclusively age his whiskey in new, charred oak barrels, and so may have created the first modern bourbon. As such, this distillery is steeped in history.

Brown-Forman owned it from 1940 until the early 1960s, then re-acquired and restored it in 1996. It is unusual in that it uses modified pot stills, made in Scotland, for all distillations instead of the column stills typically used for the first distillation at other American distilleries. The distillery's only product, Woodford Reserve bourbon, is a combination of this pot still whiskey and whiskey made at the company's Shively plant.

Buffalo Trace. The Buffalo Trace Distillery in Frankfort, Kentucky, makes several different bourbon formulas, both rye-flavored and wheat-flavored, and sells a seemingly endless array of different brands, some of them among the best in the business. Buffalo Trace is owned by the Sazerac Company, which is owned by the Goldring family.

I could recommend many Buffalo Trace products but I'll limit myself to three, their namesake rye-flavored bourbon, their superb Blanton's bourbon (also rye-flavored), and their principal wheat-flavored bourbon, W. L. Weller Special Reserve.

Anchor Distilling. Finally, Anchor Distilling of San Francisco, sister to the better known Anchor Brewery, and both owned by Fritz Maytag. The company's whiskey, Old Potrero, is made of 100 percent malted rye. It comes in two expressions, one aged about one year and the other aged about three. The 3-year-old, known as Old Potrero Straight Rye whiskey, is the one to try. If you can try it in a bar without making the considerable investment in a bottle, that is the way to go.

In addition to the whiskies made by the distilleries just described, there is some whiskey still around that was made by distilleries that are now dark. Some of it is old inventory in bottles that is still sitting in warehouses or on retailer shelves. Since straight whiskey essentially keeps forever, it is not uncommon for the odd bottle or two to sit on a shelf for twenty years or more. Combing liquor stores for forgotten gems can be a fun hobby.

The rest of the whiskey out there from defunct distilleries is whiskey acquired in the barrel by one of the active distilleries or another marketer, either on the open market or through merger. The most famous example of this is A. H. Hirsch bourbon, which is whiskey made at Pennsylvania's Michter Distillery, which closed in the late 1980s. By the time you read this, most of that whiskey will be gone. When 'orphan' whiskey like that is bottled and made available for sale, it usually is in a very limited supply. All of this makes it hard for me to point you in the right direction in terms of trying some.

The type of whiskey just described—genuine finds from closed plants—should not be confused with the products that appear in your local liquor store attributed to 'The Old So-and-So Distillery,' a name you can't find in the index of this book. In most cases, these are either products of the distilleries listed above, operating under a d.b.a. ('doing business as') name, or products marketed by third parties using bulk whiskey produced by one of the distilleries listed above. Many, if not most, of the distillery names used are invented for the occasion. Some of the products are good, some not. Often they feature fancy packaging and indifferent whisky. Only rarely are they the 'discoveries' they purport or may appear to be.

Chapter Nine

How Whiskey Won the West (and the Movies).

After the Civil War, new railroads carried bourbon whiskey west to the new frontier and the era of large, commercial distilleries began. This period also brought with it a large, permanent Federal Excise Tax on distilled spirits. If there is anything good to say about the excise tax it is that it got cowboys to pay taxes. Because the tax was paid by producers, it was built into the price of every shot of whiskey poured at the Long Branch and dozens of other cowtown saloons strung along the Atchison, Topeka and Santa Fe; Kansas Pacific; and Union Pacific railroad tracks.

The historical period known as the Wild West began after the Civil War when veterans, mostly Rebels who had little waiting for them at home, learned that vast herds of longhorn cattle were wandering wild all across northern Texas, abandoned there in the chaos following Mexico's separation from

Spain (1821), the War of Texas Independence (1832-1836) and the Mexican War (1846-1848). The cattle were unbranded, unclaimed and there for the taking. All you had to do was round some up and get them to Kansas, where railroads were just beginning to pierce the eastern edge of the western frontier. The trains would take the cattle on to the slaughterhouses of Chicago. Just as these eastbound trains were full of beef, westbound trains were full of whiskey for the thirsty cowboys. Whiskey at the time cost two to four dollars a gallon and the typical cowboy was paid about $30 a month, so the economics worked out just fine.

Although his pay was poor the cowboy's needs were modest. An 1871 Kansas newspaper described the typical cowboy as "unlearned and illiterate, with few wants and meager ambition," who lives on a "diet of Navy plug and whisky." An 1884 visitor to Dodge City noted that, "The cowboy spends his money recklessly. He is a jovial, careless fellow bent on having a big time regardless of expense. He will make away with the wages of a half year in a few weeks, and then go back to his herds for another six months."

The cowboy in town with money in his pockets had three entertainment options: the saloon which featured whiskey, women, and gambling; the dance hall which featured whiskey, women, and music; and the brothel which concentrated on whiskey and women.

The first commercial structure erected at the site of what became Dodge City, Kansas, was a tent saloon for buffalo hunters, put up years before the arrival of thirsty cowboys and their scraggly longhorn steers. By 1876, Dodge was a town of 1,200 souls and 19 licensed whiskey-selling establishments. The population swelled during the summer, of course, from all the traffic on the Western Trail. In addition to the Long Branch (made famous by the "Gunsmoke" TV series), other saloons on Dodge's Front Street included the Alhambra, the Alamo, the Old House Saloon, the Opera House Saloon, the Junction Saloon, and the Green Front. Whiskey was the principal drink served at all of these establishments. Beer did not appear in Dodge until about 1879. In one probably typical year, Dodge City's residents and guests consumed 300 barrels of whiskey. If there were 3,000 drinkers in town that year, a reasonable estimate between residents and transients, that is about 5.5 gallons for each.

The saloons also sold food. Here is a typical scene: A cowboy calls out his order for a sandwich and some Limburger cheese as he drops into a chair and swings his feet onto the table. The bartender brings the order and places it next to the cowboy's feet. Soon the cowboy is complaining, "This cheese is no good; I can't smell it." The bartender replies, "Put your feet down and give the cheese a chance." (An example of cowboy humor.)

The actual, historical 'Wild West' lasted barely 30 years and involved a few thousand individuals but it has fed the imaginations of Americans and people around the world ever since. It has been portrayed in literature, music, painting and sculpture, and perhaps most of all in TV and film westerns. Westerns are often criticized for their historical inaccuracy, but to the extent they show ubiquitous drinking and saloons, they are realistic. John Ford's classic "Stagecoach" (1939)—the movie that made John Wayne a star—

features a meek character (played by an actor named Donald Meek) who is a whiskey drummer (i.e., a traveling whiskey salesman). His name is Mr. Peacock. Before the stagecoach reaches its final destination, the lovable but permanently parched Doc Boone (played by Thomas Mitchell) has worked his way through Mr. Peacock's entire case of whiskey samples. In "Stagecoach," every stop along the trail has a bar, even the smallest inn. In the fancy saloon at the end of the line, where the bad guys learn that Ringo (Wayne) is coming, hot for revenge, the bartenders sense trouble and immediately remove a large gilded mirror from behind the bar, so as to protect it from destruction in the ensuing melee.

In the Alan Ladd epic "Shane" (1953), about half of the movie (and all of the action) takes place in Grafton's General Mercantile Co. Sundries and Saloon, where the mean cowboys (led by Jack Palance's 'Jack Wilson') loll around all day drinking whiskey and taunting sod busters until Shane gives them what for. The typical bar call in most of these westerns is just 'whiskey,' never 'bourbon.' Sometimes the character just says, "Bring me a bottle." In "The Plainsman" (1937), Gary Cooper's Wild Bill Hickok orders 'rye' as he joins a riverboat card game. Two of his fellow players order the same and the third asks for applejack. Later in the film, when the town dandy asks for a 'sherry and egg' he gets whiskey and egg. The joke is that the whiskey costs two bits (25 cents) but the hard-boiled egg costs a dollar. When Brynner buys McQueen a drink at the beginning of "The Magnificent Seven" (1960) he orders whiskey. In "High Noon" (1952), no one has to say a word. They just walk up to the bar and the bartender sets down the shot glass and bottle.

Although the term wasn't used, was it, in fact, bourbon whiskey served in those frontier saloons? Maybe. It was, at the very least, some sort of American whiskey. Scotch had not yet made it to the Great Plains. The big producers for the western markets were the Kentucky, Tennessee and Illinois distilleries whose primary product was bourbon. What they sent West may have started out as bourbon, but often something bad happened to it along the way. Various 'extenders' were added, if not by distributors then by the saloon keepers themselves. At the end of the day, most of the cowboys didn't know nor care, as long as one of the ingredients in the mixture was alcohol.

While we're on the subject of bar calls, the generic 'whiskey' may have been acceptable in the Old West, but in Kentucky you are expected to be more specific. There was one U.S. senator from there who, when in Louisville, took his lunch each afternoon in the bar at the august Pendennis Club. Being an accomplished politician, he had a standing arrangement with the bartender. When the senator entered the room he would hail the man loudly and request 'the usual.' The bartender would then surreptitiously scan the room, determine which local bourbon distiller was present, and pour the senator a few fingers of that man's brand. One day the senator performed his trick and was surprised to receive a gin and tonic. Before he could spit out the vile potion and express his outrage, the bartender leaned over and whispered in his ear, "Sorry, Senator, but they're *all* here." In Kentucky, drinking only bourbon is a matter of local pride. One

Louisville bar still has a sign that reads, "Gentlemen imbibing foreign and alien spirits other than Bourbon whiskey may be requested to pay in cash."

But back to the movies, it isn't just in westerns that people drink. Where movie cowboys seldom order more than 'whiskey,' today's tough guys often specify a brand. This comes in part from the practice of movie placement, in which a marketer pays a producer for using a particular brand in a film. When Kevin Kostner gets drunk on Jim Beam in "Bull Durham" (1988), it isn't so much about character development as brand development. Likewise in "Spider-Man" (2002), when the rich villain Norman Osborn (Willem Dafoe) pours himself a Maker's Mark. In "French Connection II" (1975), Gene Hackman struggles with the language barrier in Paris as he first orders "Four Roses straight up, water on the side," then switches to Jack Daniel's, and finally settles for 'whisky' which, he discovers to his chagrin, outside the U.S. automatically means scotch. In "It's A Wonderful Life" (1946), Frank Capra has George Bailey (Jimmy Stewart) order a 'double bourbon' to signify his despair. On the TV show "Dallas," J. R. Ewing (Larry Hagman) always ordered 'bourbon and branch,' 'branch' being a word that meant something in the 18th century but is now just a pretentious way to say 'water.'

Robert Rossen was one producer/director who had a good handle on what his characters should drink. One quick exchange in "All The King's Men" (1949) has politician Willy Stark (Broderick Crawford) ordering "double bourbon," followed by a rapid fire "same for me" from his female aide, played by Mercedes McCambridge (who won an Oscar for that role but, presumably, not for that line). Rossen was heavy-handed with symbolism and the hearty drinking in "All The King's Men" signifies the growing corruption of Stark's political movement. Whiskey was a metaphor for weakness and lack of self control in Rossen's "The Hustler" (1961). 'Fast' Eddie Felson (Paul Newman) drinks J.T.S. Brown bourbon, straight from the bottle, during the film's climactic pool duel. His opponent, Minnesota Fats (Jackie Gleason), requests "White Tavern Whiskey, a glass and some ice." We are left to consider the possibility that Fats' brand is actually a placebo, a way to keep his advantage over Eddie by staying sober.

The change from the old westerns to the movies of today mirrors the change in the role and status of American whiskey in American culture. Where American whiskey was ubiquitous but generic in the westerns, today it is only one of many possible beverage choices, but when it does appear it is branded and specific almost to the point of cliché. The best known and most emblematic American whiskey is Jack Daniel's and, sure enough, the folks at Jack Daniel's have counted 86 motion pictures in which their product has appeared since 1963. That list can be found on the internet at http://www.jackdaniels.com /jackinmovies.asp.

Chapter Ten

Whiskey, War and Taxes.

Whiskey, taxes and war have been partners for as long as there has been a United States. Federal excise taxes on distilled spirits were first imposed in 1791 to pay off long overdue Revolutionary War debts. They were the young republic's first internal revenue tax, before which the government had been entirely funded by import duties. The much-reviled tax was abolished in 1802 but reinstated briefly after the War of 1812. In 1862 it was reinstated again to pay for the Civil War, after which it became permanent. During that war, the excise tax produced one-quarter of the federal government's total income. By 1876, liquor taxes were generating fully one-half of federal revenue, a level of contribution that continued for more than 30 years, until the eve of Prohibition. The fact that the federal government gave up such a rich revenue stream makes the adoption of National Prohibition even more surprising. It is no coincidence that Congress passed the first income tax in 1913 to make up for the expected revenue loss. In 1933, with war threatening again, one rationale for repealing Prohibition was to regain a lucrative revenue stream to pay for defense.

Although the whiskey industry has paid a lot of taxes, in part to fund the military, it got some of that money back in the early days of the Republic, when both the Army and Navy provided a daily spirits ration to all soldiers and sailors. From 1794 until 1842, the Navy's daily ration was one-half pint. It was reduced to one-quarter pint in 1842 and abolished twenty years later. The Army's spirits ration, similar in size to the Navy's during and after the Revolution, was abolished in 1832 by executive order of President Andrew Jackson. The order specifically substituted coffee, which remains part of the American soldier's provisions to this day.

In July of 1940, more than a year before Pearl Harbor (but with war clearly on the horizon), the Federal Excise Tax on Distilled Spirits (FET) was increased from $2.25 per proof gallon to $3.00 per proof gallon, expressly for the purpose of funding a defense buildup. (A 'proof gallon' is one gallon of 100 proof whiskey.) The new rate was billed as 'temporary' and indeed it was, because in October of 1941, the rate was raised again to $4.00 per proof gallon and made permanent. In November of 1942, it went to $6.00 per proof gallon, where it remained for just 17 months. In April of 1944, it was raised to $9.00 per proof gallon. That increase was supposed to be temporary but it officially became permanent in March of 1947.

World War II was fundamentally different from everything we have called a war since. It was a total war, a battle for basic survival. Fighting it required a complete mobilization of every part of society and the government required more from the distilling industry than its tax payments. War industries didn't need whiskey, they needed industrial alcohol, i.e., 190+ proof grain neutral spirits (GNS). The largest whiskey plants were retrofitted so they could produce it directly. The rest were ordered to distill out as high as their equipment allowed, say 160 proof, then that spirit was shipped to other plants where it was redistilled into industrial grade alcohol.

The alcohol the whiskey industry produced was used in many essential war industries such as the production of synthetic rubber (650 million gallons), explosives (102 million gallons), fuel (66 million gallons), anti-freeze (126 million gallons), plastics (75 million gallons), textiles (70 million gallons), other chemicals (115 million gallons) and drugs (30 million gallons). Whiskey that had been made in prior years, that was aging in rackhouses when the war began, was directed to the military services for medicinal use.

After the war, the FET continued to rise. Currently it is $13.50 per proof gallon. Most states and some cities levy additional taxes on spirits, either on the basis of volume or value. According to the Distilled Spirits Council, taxes make up 44 percent of the price of a typical bottle of whiskey or other distilled spirit.

From the earliest days, enforcement of the FET has taken a large bureaucracy. It has always been in the Treasury Department, for a long time as part of the Internal Revenue Service (IRS) and now as part of the Alcohol, Tobacco and Firearms Bureau (ATF). The tax is based on the volume of production and the proof of the whiskey produced, and especially in the early days there were thousands of small distilleries to monitor. Moonshiners called enforcement agents 'revenuers,' legitimate distillers called them 'government men,' and they were a fixture at every distillery. The government man had two main jobs, often combined in the title 'storekeeper and gauger.' In his storekeeper capacity, he controlled access to all of the plant's grain bins, stills and warehouses. In his gauger capacity, he monitored the proof of whiskey coming off the still.

Paul Civils, now in his 80s, was one of the last government men in Kentucky. When he joined the IRS in 1966 there were 50 people working out of the Bardstown office, monitoring distilleries in Nelson and surrounding counties. Today there is only one. "We had lock and key charge of the distillery operations because the tax had to be paid if whiskey left the premises," says Civils. Because the government man controlled all access to the distillery, literally unlocking the doors each morning and locking them again at quitting time, distillery owners and their workers were at his mercy. If a distiller angered an agent in some way, that agent might be a little late for work the next morning, costing the distiller thousands of dollars in lost production. "Some of the old guys had a policeman attitude," says Civils. "But when I was there it wasn't bad. They moved us around to different places to prevent those problems." The system of having Treasury agents control access to the distilleries, in place for a century, was abolished in the early 1980s. "Today it's all a post audit, done with computers," says Civils.

Today, the whiskey ration for soldiers and sailors is gone. So is the ubiquitous government man. But war and taxes are still with us and, thankfully, as a small compensation, so is the whiskey that funds them.

Chapter Eleven

Even the River Was Burning.

In June of 1969, an oil slick caught fire on the Cuyahoga River just southeast of downtown Cleveland, Ohio. I am from a small city about 60 miles south of Cleveland and my mother was a Clevelander. My Indians weren't doing very well that summer either. This was not the first nor only time the Cuyahoga River had burned. There had been a much larger fire there in 1952, but this time the story received national attention and became a powerful symbol both for the scourge of water pollution and the decline of Cleveland and other rust belt cities.

I thought about the Cuyahoga when a small creek south of Bardstown caught on fire on November 7, 1996. The burning creek was just one small part of a spectacular conflagration that consumed two percent of the world's total supply of aging bourbon whiskey, along with a 60-year-old distillery and other facilities at Heaven Hill. Throughout that afternoon and into the evening, flaming streams of burning bourbon flowed like molten lava and the fire's intense heat could be felt half a mile away. Flames leapt hundreds of feet into the air and lit the sky throughout the night. Witnesses reported seeing whiskey barrels explode and rocket across the sky like shooting stars. It was the worst distillery fire in decades and *every* distillery fire is terrible. Luckily, no one was seriously injured.

Although its exact cause was never determined, the Heaven Hill fire started in one of the distillery's rackhouses and quickly spread to six others. Seven rackhouses and their contents were completely destroyed and the distillery itself was damaged beyond repair. In addition, three grain trucks and their loads were lost. High winds and streams of flaming whiskey helped spread the fire and a two-mile long stretch of the creek that supplied process water to the distillery was set ablaze for a brief time. State officials later said the environmental impact of the fire had been minimal.

The approximately 7.7 million gallons of aging bourbon that were destroyed that day represented about two percent of all the bourbon in the world. Fortunately, the company's proprietary yeast strain, which it had used since 1935, was saved. Fires are a constant danger in a distillery, and have been since frontier times. Although elaborate precautions are taken with electrical connections and other potential sources of sparks, distillery fires can never be completely prevented. Kentucky's climate seems unusually prone to electrical storms and lightning strikes are a frequent cause of distillery fires. The rackhouses at Heaven Hill were a typical design, a framework of wood covered by a thin, metal skin. Each rackhouse contained thousands of oak barrels, saturated with a liquid that is about 60 percent absolute alcohol. In other words, a whiskey rackhouse and everything in it is extremely combustible. As in all distillery fires, the affected buildings were simply allowed to burn as firefighters concentrated on preventing any further spread of the blaze. Considering the nature of the fuel involved, any effort to actually extinguish a rackhouse fire would be futile.

Ironically, the Heaven Hill site was believed to be one of the least likely to experience a massive fire of this sort because of its design. The rackhouses are spaced very far apart. Unusually high winds helped the fire bridge the gap between buildings, as did the fact that the first warehouse to burn was above the others on the hill, allowing escaping, flaming whiskey to flow downhill and carry its destruction to the buildings below. Once the fire got going, everything in its path was doomed. The distillery building itself was located at the lowest point in the terrain, close to the water source, so its destruction was inevitable.

At the time of the Heaven Hill blaze, many commentators said they could not recall a previous distillery fire. In fact, it had been almost 25 years since the last one. The next one would be much sooner than that. The 1972 event was at the Athertonville Distillery in LaRue County, near New Haven. The Athertonville plant was then owned by Seagrams. A fire broke out there at 3:40 AM on Saturday, February 19. No one was hurt. Everything inside the brick distillery building was destroyed, including grain bins and mills, mash tubs and stills. The fermenting room, power house and evaporator were spared, as were the three rackhouses on the site. The fire was believed to have been started by a spark from the milling system. The plant, on the site along Knob Creek where Abraham Lincoln's father was once employed as a distillery hand, never reopened. Today it is a small cooperage.

You have to go back another quarter century to find the fire before that one. On the morning of June 1, 1945, fire destroyed the distillery plant and fermenting room at the Barton Distillery in Bardstown. Barton had only recently taken over and renamed what had been the Tom Moore Distillery. The fire began in an alcohol pump that had been giving the staff trouble all day, and it soon enveloped the building. Six thousand bushels of stored grain were also lost. The plant had been producing GNS for the war effort. In addition to 60 employees put temporarily out of work by the fire, approximately 200 local farmers who relied on slop from the distillery for cattle feed were affected. A special train of ten cars was sent to Bardstown the next day to take 237 head of cattle to feedlots in Louisville. Eventually, 4,000 head of cattle and a large number of hogs had to be shipped to feedlots or to market as a consequence of the fire. The distillery was rebuilt and reopened, and continues to operate to this day.

After the Heaven Hill fire in 1996, it was less than four years before another whiskey rackhouse went up in flames, this time at Wild Turkey in Lawrenceburg. That fire began in the afternoon of May 9, 2000. Only one rackhouse was affected, but it was destroyed within 90 minutes. No one was injured, although two firefighters were treated for heat exhaustion. As much as one million gallons of bourbon was lost. Burning whiskey flowed into the Kentucky River, threatening the local drinking water supply. Normal water service was restored two days later.

By the end of the week it seemed as if the fire, while a major loss to the company, had caused little environmental harm. Then reports began to emerge of a large fish kill in the river. One week after the fire, on May 16, officials of the Kentucky Department of Fish and Wildlife Resources announced that a 28-mile-long 'dead zone' was floating down the Kentucky River with the current, killing everything in its path. Officials speculated that algae had fed on the alcohol and then depleted the water of oxygen. The next day, the size of the deadly plume was re-estimated as four to five miles long, moving downstream at a rate of five miles per day. It would become the worst fish kill in Kentucky history. All species in the river were affected, including paddlefish, catfish, shiner minnows, spoonbills, carp, gar and saugers. Although at first officials were not sure the Wild Turkey spill had caused the problem, observers reported that the deadly plume had a distinct bourbon-like odor.

By the following week, the Coast Guard had hit on a clever solution. Equipment mounted on barges was used to blow bubbles into the water, aerating it. Two compressors, six pumps and five aerators were used. Wild Turkey paid about $300,000 for the work. State officials subsequently estimated that 227,000 fish died as a result of the accident. They presented Wild Turkey with a bill for $471,000 for the fish, and $28,000 in investigative expenses and costs. Company officials immediately contested the damage assessment. As for the cause of the fire, distillery employees told investigators that the building had been listing badly and was scheduled to be repaired. Investigators speculated that it had collapsed and the fire started as a result.

The most recent distillery fire struck Jim Beam in October of 2003, again destroying one rackhouse, with a loss of approximately 800,000 gallons of whiskey. It occurred at one of the many rackhouse locations Beam uses at sites of defunct distilleries. The two Beam distilleries themselves were never at risk. No one was injured in this fire either, which was believed to have been started by lightning. Once again, though, a small creek was ignited and had to be dammed by firefighters to prevent the fire from spreading further. Three fires in less than ten years may seem like a lot, but there are approximately 200 whiskey rackhouses spread across Kentucky and they are extremely flammable. In 2001, Wild Turkey built a new rackhouse to replace the one it had lost. When Heaven Hill acquired the Bernheim distillery, it also gained several masonry rackhouses on that site. It is using them to age brandy, not bourbon.

In addition to fires, whiskey has been lost through other natural disasters. In 1974, Jim Beam lost several rackhouses when a tornado swept through the area and struck their Boston facility. Naturally, all of these losses have been insured and although the FET is technically assessed when whiskey leaves the still, it is waived in the event of a fire or other disaster.

Chapter Twelve

The Ubiquitous Beams.

It is hard to imagine another major American industry that has been as dominated by one family as the American whiskey industry has been by the Beams. The involvement of families across multiple generations has been a hallmark of this industry and other families—the Dants, Browns, Samuels, Wathens, Medleys, Bixlers, Ripys, Ices, Moores, Motlows, Peppers, Van Winkles, and others—have significant histories too. But no other family can compare to the Beams in sheer numbers, nor in the number of different companies affected. In part, this is because the clan is simply huge. Generation after generation, Beam families with ten or more children have been common. In an industry that is so close knit and concentrated, it also isn't surprising that most of the other prominent families are connected to the Beams by marriage.

In addition to fecundity, another difference be-tween the Beams and some of the other families has been that while many of the others were prominent primarily as distillery proprietors, most of the Beams have been hands-on whiskey-makers. While members of the Beam family have owned a plant or two, they are most notable as the whiskey-making employees of others, including at the company that still bears the family name. And they have not been limited to Kentucky. Everett Beam was master distiller at the Michter Distillery in Pennsylvania. Charlie Beam worked for Seagrams in Baltimore. Otis Beam worked at a distillery in Indiana. During Prohibition, Joe and Harry Beam operated a distillery in Mexico, while Guy Beam ran one in Canada.

All of the whiskey-making Beams trace their lineage back to Johannes Jacob Boehm, a Pennsylvanian of German descent who came to Kentucky by way of Maryland and, along the way, Americanized his name to Jake Beam. He was a miller and distiller, a common combination in those days. Jacob and his wife, Mary, had twelve children. By 1795, they were in Kentucky and he was making whiskey alongside one of his sons, David. This is where the line splits, because this David Beam (who had eleven children) had three sons who made whiskey, as did many of their progeny. The three whiskey-makers were, in order of birth, Joseph B. Beam, David M. Beam and John H. 'Jack' Beam.

It is interesting to note that memories run long in bourbon country. The many Beams still living in Nelson and surrounding counties count each other as cousins, even though in some cases their nearest common ancestor died 150 years ago. Such is the fame of the name and its connection to the region's most famous industry.

The oldest and most prolific of the sons of David Beam was Joseph B., born in 1825. We don't know much about him except that he lived to be 91, he and his wife, Mary Ellen, had fourteen children. and two of their sons became prominent as whiskey-makers. We don't know where Joseph himself made whiskey, but presumably it was at the family's distillery in Washington County, where he would have worked with his father and brothers. It is possible he kept his whiskey-making activities off the books, as many did. Anything is possible, because we just don't know, but considering what came before and especially what came after, it is hard to imagine he didn't make his living off his skill with a still.

We do know quite a bit about his two whiskey-making sons. The first was Minor Case Beam. (When you have 14 kids, at least one odd name is inevitable.) He worked at several places before buying an interest in the F. M. Head Distillery at Gethsemane, in southern Nelson County, which he eventually renamed the M. C. Beam Distillery. In 1910, he sold out to J. B. Dant, who owned the distillery next door and wanted to use both plants to make his popular Yellowstone bourbon, which was named after the national park. Minor's son, Guy, worked at several Kentucky distilleries before and after Prohibition. *During* Prohibition he ran a Canadian distillery for the Wathen family's American Medicinal Spirits Company, where he made Old Crow and Old Grand-Dad, presumably for surreptitious export back into the USA. Guy and his wife, Mary, had ten children. One of their sons, Jack, worked at the

Barton Distillery in Bardstown. Another son, Walter (known as Toddy), owned Bardstown's most popular liquor store, which is still called Toddy's today.

The other son of Joseph B. Beam who worked in the whiskey business was his namesake, Joseph L., who had a long career as a distiller and also produced seven distiller sons. If Joseph L. Beam and his 'boys' had been the only Beams in the whiskey business, it still would be an amazing story. Joe Beam's first distillery job, at age 14, was at his Uncle Jack's place, Early Times. At age 19, Joe became master distiller at his older brother's Gethsemane plant. After that he worked at several other distilleries, some simultaneously, including Tom Moore and Mattingly & Moore, which were both located where the Barton Distillery is today, and S. P. Lancaster, which at one point was owned by Tom Pendergast, the notorious political boss of Kansas City. When Prohibition arrived, Joe was master distiller and part owner at F. G. Walker, whose president at the time was his cousin, Jim Beam.

Joe Beam's 'boys,' his seven distiller sons, were born between 1895 and 1910, so they mostly missed the pre-Prohibition industry. During Prohibition, Joe took his son Harry, who was still a child, with him to Juarez, Mexico, where he set up and ran a distillery for an old Kentucky whiskey concern, Waterfill & Frazier. They took apart the Kentucky plant, carted the pieces to Mexico, and reassembled it there. Harry (full name Henry Milburn Beam), born in 1910, was the youngest of the seven brothers. The others, in birth order, were Joseph Elmo, known as Elmo, born 1895; Roy Marion, known as Roy, born 1898; Frederic Otis, known as Otis, born 1900; Wilmer Bernard, known as Wilmer, born 1903; Desmond Aloysius, known as Desmond, born 1905; and Charles Everett, known as Everett, born 1907.

By 1929, Joe and Harry had returned from Mexico, and Joe had won election as Nelson County's jailer. That December, Joe and Roy became the first distillers to legally make whiskey in the United States since the advent of Prohibition. Not only was the A. Ph. Stitzel plant in Louisville one of the few distilleries with a medicinal whiskey license, it was also one of the few with an operable distillery. In 1929, with medicinal stocks running low (and repeal looking increasingly probable), the federal government gave Stitzel permission to fire up its stills and, naturally, the Stitzel family called in the Beams to do the job. After Prohibition, Stitzel merged with its primary customer, the W. L. Weller Company, to form Stitzel-Weller. Joe Beam's brother-in-law, Will McGill, was hired as Stitzel-Weller's master distiller. McGill had come up with Joe Beam at Early Times and Tom Moore. At one time or another in the decades that followed repeal, Uncle Will employed most of his Beam nephews at Stitzel-Weller.

When Prohibition ended, Joe Beam (aka 'Pops') wanted a distillery of his own. With several other veteran Nelson County distillers he founded the Old Heaven Hill Spring Distillery, but they were undercapitalized and gradually had to sell out. Even so, Joe Beam was vital to Heaven Hill's operations for its first decade of existence. He supervised construction of the distillery in 1934, installed young Harry as distiller, and oversaw all of the whiskey-making there until he retired in 1945. Harry left the next year after a dispute with management. By 1949, Harry was in financial difficulty and got caught making moonshine, a great embarrassment to his mother, Katherine McGill Beam, who had enough clout to keep it out of the local newspaper. Harry's daughter, Jo Ann Beam, finally outed him in a History Channel documentary in 2002. Jo Ann Beam worked in the bottling house at Jim Beam for 38 years and is responsible for preserving much of the family's history.

While he was getting Heaven Hill started, Joe Beam also was helping his son, Roy, get the stills going over at the new Frankfort Distillery in Louisville, which made Four Roses bourbon. Roy was master distiller there, assisted by his father and two of his brothers, Otis and Wilmer. In addition to his 'boys,' Joe brought with him to Frankfort the precious yeast strain he had been using at various places since 1895. Roy stayed at Frankfort and two of his sons, Charlie (Charles Lloyd Beam) and Jack (John Dugan Beam), joined him there. Ownership of Frankfort passed to Seagrams. When they closed it after the war, Roy went to Park & Tilford with Charlie, who later went back to work for Seagrams at their Baltimore plant. While with Seagrams, Charlie created the Eagle Rare bourbon brand. He ended his career in 1982 at the Lawrenceburg distillery that makes Four Roses today.

Roy Beam's other son, Jack, moved to the nearby Yellowstone plant where his Uncle Wilmer had been installed as master distiller. At Park & Tilford, which was owned by Schenley, Roy was in charge of two Kentucky distilleries, at Louisville and Midway

(Woodford County), as well as distilleries in Brownsville, Pennsylvania; Owings Mills, Maryland; and Tell City, Indiana (where the Park & Tilford name originated). His brother Desmond worked for him at Midway and his other brother, Otis, was at Tell City. Between their stints at Frankfort and Park & Tilford, Otis had been at Buffalo Springs and Desmond had been at Old Kennebec.

Another of the brothers, Everett Beam, worked for his Uncle Will at Stitzel-Weller, then for a time at a distillery in Cleveland, Ohio, then for 40 years as master distiller at the Michter Distillery in Pennsylvania. After it closed in 1988, some of the whiskey made there was rescued and transferred to stainless steel to prevent it from over-aging. It has been bottled and sold in recent years under the A. H. Hirsch name and is considered a superb bourbon.

The oldest of the seven brothers, Elmo, had a long association with the Samuels family, first at their T. W. Samuels plant near Bardstown and later at Maker's Mark, which he helped build and worked at until his death in 1955. One year later, death also ended the long career of his father, at age 88. Roy passed in 1959. He was followed by Harry in 1971, Otis in 1975, Wilmer in 1977, Desmond in 1981, and Everett in 1989. It is perhaps a symbol of how diminished the American whiskey industry has become that no descendant of Joe Beam is making whiskey anywhere today.

At this point in our story we have only just covered the eldest son of David Beam. We still have two sons to go. David's middle son was his namesake, David M. Beam. Born in 1833, David worked with his father and brothers at the family's distillery in Washington

County. Their father died in 1852 and a few years later, in 1860, David decided to relocate the distillery to Nelson County, to be close to the new railroad tracks. It is not known if his older brother, Joseph, was still involved with the company at this time, but David seems to have been the one in charge. We do know that his younger brother, Jack, in that same year decided to start his own whiskey company on the same railroad line, about four miles away from David's new plant.

The coming of the railroad made a huge impact on the region's distillers. It allowed whiskey to be shipped to more distant markets and made it practical for distillers to sell more of their output directly to customers (that is, to taverns and shopkeepers) instead of exclusively to distributor middlemen. Selling directly to distant customers made brand names more important and the creation of many famous whiskey brand names coincides with the arrival of the railroad. David Beam called his bourbon 'Old Tub.' David's subsequent brands were given more evocative names such as 'Clear Springs' and 'Pebbleford.'

Two of this David's four sons also became distillers. The older of the two was James Beauregard 'Jim' Beam, born in 1864, who would become the most famous Beam of them all. Jim and his younger brother, Park, took over the family business in 1892, along with their sister's husband, Albert J. Hart. By this time the distillery had a mashing capacity of 150 bushels of grain per day and their four rackhouses could store up to 10,000 barrels of aging whiskey. They operated this distillery until Prohibition closed it. As Prohibition approached, Jim also bought a controlling interest in the F. G. Walker plant where his cousin, Joe, was master distiller and a part-owner.

Jim Beam married Mary Catherine Montgomery in 1897. Uncharacteristically for the Beams, Jim and Mary Catherine had just three children; a son, T. Jeremiah, and two daughters, Mildred and Margaret. As soon as he was old enough (about 13), 'Jerry' (they spelled it 'Jere' but pronounced it 'Jerry') went to work at the distillery. His sister, Margaret, married Frederick Booker Noe and one of their sons, Booker Jr., went to work there too. He would eventually oversee the Jim Beam Company distillery at Boston, Kentucky, and become world famous as the company's spokesperson, a role that is now being taken over by his son, Fred (formally Frederick Booker Noe III).

During Prohibition, Jim Beam and his family were involved in several non-distilling businesses, none very successful, including a gravel quarry at the site of the old Murphy, Barber & Co. Distillery at Clermont, in Bullitt County. When Prohibition ended, Jim (age 70), Park (66) and their sons rounded up some investors and built a new distillery at the Clermont site, which was on the same railroad line as their former plant, but several miles nearer to the main line. They resurrected the Old Tub brand, adding to it a new bourbon called simply 'Jim Beam.' Jere ran the business side and Park's two sons, Carl (known as 'Shucks') and Earl, made the whiskey. Park was first to leave, to become master distiller at the Willett Distilling Company. Jim Beam retired in 1944 and died in 1947. One of his pall bearers was T. W. Samuels, his next door neighbor, close friend, friendly competitor, and grandfather of current Maker's Mark president Bill Samuels Jr.

After World War II, Harry Blum, son of one of the original investors, bought out the other owners. In 1967, Blum sold the company to American Tobacco, which changed its name to American Brands and today is known as Fortune Brands. Shucks Beam remained as master distiller and lived in a house on the distillery property. He retired in 1974. His sons, Baker and David, succeeded him at Clermont. Baker, the oldest, supervised the day shift and David supervised the night shift. Baker retired in 1992, followed by David in 1996.

In 1946, when Harry Beam left Heaven Hill, Earl Beam left his job at Jim Beam, where he was his younger brother's assistant, and took the master distiller's job at Heaven Hill. Earl was succeeded there by his son, Parker, who with his son, Craig, makes Heaven Hill's whiskey today. The Beams at Jim Beam and their cousins at Heaven Hill were always friendly competitors, regularly swapping equipment and parts, and helping each other whenever needed. At times, the two companies have deliberately bought the same equipment to make parts swaps easier. It has always been that way among the Beams.

The youngest of the three whiskey-making sons of David Beam was John Henry 'Jack' Beam, born in 1839. Only 13 when his father died, Jack worked with his older brothers at the family distillery until he turned 21, then he built his own plant, calling it Early Times. The name was a reference to certain old fashioned practices he favored, such as using small, hand-stirred tubs for mashing and open fires, not steam, to boil his beer in pot stills instead of the more common column stills. Jack lost financial control of his company during the Panic of 1880 but stayed on as master distiller until his death in 1915. Even without full ownership, the plant seems to have made the family prosperous. Jack had a 1,000 acre farm close to the distillery property. His son, Edward, bred racehorses and had 60 of them at one time. Sadly, Edward was Jack's only son and had no offspring of his own. He died, at age 42, a few months before his father passed, at age 76.

Jack Beam had a close relationship with his nephew, Jim Beam, who was a few years older than Edward. Jack was best man at Jim's wedding. Their distilleries were just a few miles apart along the Bardstown Branch of the L&N Railroad. By the time Prohibition arrived, Early Times had become a very successful bourbon. In 1923, Brown-Forman bought the name, but not the distillery, which never reopened. In the 1950s, Brown-Forman built a new distillery south of Louisville and named it Early Times. Their Early Times Kentucky whiskey continues to be a leading seller today.

So far as is known, all of the many Beams have been practical distillers, which means the yeast they use is propagated from a wild strain. The alternative is scientific distilling, in which a pure strain yeast bred in a laboratory and manufactured in a factory is used. With pure strain yeast, every spore is identical and such yeasts can be manufactured in dry form. In contrast, wild yeast is also known as 'jug yeast' because it must be kept in a liquid medium and constantly tended lest an undesirable strain take over and spoil it. A practical distiller will mix his special medium and then capture a suitable yeast from the air. This can be a very hit-or-miss proposition. Booker Noe often told the story of his grandfather "stinking up the house" while trying to propagate a suitable yeast at the end of Prohibition.

Of the Beam family members active in recent decades, the best known has been Booker Noe, who died on February 24, 2004, at the age of 74. Booker started working at the distillery named for his grandfather in 1951 and rose to be master distiller at the company's second plant in Boston, Kentucky, a job he held for 32 years. As master distiller, Booker was expected to monitor the bourbon aging in the company's rackhouses and was able to help himself to any whiskey that interested him in that vast network. He found that for his personal consumption, he favored bourbon from his plant that had been aged for between six and eight years. He took it straight from the barrel, at about 126 proof, usually running it into a 1.75 liter Jim Beam white label bottle to take home. Because it came straight from the barrel, the whiskey was not filtered, as most bourbon is prior to bottling. This was, literally, 'Booker's Bourbon' long before there was a product by that name.

In 1987, Beam Company executives were looking for an unusual Christmas gift for their customers and suppliers. One of the executives had tasted Booker's private stock and suggested a special, limited bottling of Booker's special whiskey that would include a message from Booker. The gift was so successful, wholesale customers virtually demanded that the company introduce it as a product, which they did the following year. This led to Booker's role as spokesperson for Booker's Bourbon and the three other super-premium bourbons Beam released as the Small Batch Collection. (One of the others was a parallel personal bourbon that Booker's cousin, Baker Beam, selected from rackhouses at Clermont.) Naturally witty and likable, Booker was surprisingly good at public speaking and interview-giving. He had an unhurried, home-spun style that perfectly suited the brand. After he retired from active distilling in 1992, Booker continued to be a globetrotting spokesperson for the company. His son, Fred, was gradually assuming that role as Booker's health declined and with his father's death he has become the company's sole link to its Beam heritage. An heir to that throne, Frederick Booker Noe IV, is already in the wings. Like any crown prince, the young gentleman has a job waiting for him whenever he wants it.

Back in 1937, four years after Prohibition ended, there were 61 distilleries operating in Kentucky, according to a document prepared that year for tax purposes. That document lists six Beams as master distillers, as well as four Bixlers, three Ices and two Dants. No other surname appears more than once. The six Beams shown are Carl Beam, James B. Beam Distilling Co.; F. Otis Beam, Buffalo Springs Distilling Co.; Joe L. Beam, Old Heaven Hill Spring Dist. Co.; Desmond Beam, Old Kennebec Distillery Co.; Wilmer Beam, Old Kentucky Distilling Co.; and Park Beam, Willett Distilling Company.

In most of America, the ancient tradition of passing a trade from parent to child has been lost, but it lives on in at least parts of the Beam family. Booker and Fred carried on the tradition at Jim Beam. Parker and Craig

Beam seem firmly ensconced at Heaven Hill, where a granddaughter of Harry Beam also works as a bottling line mechanic. David Beam and his sons—Troy, Bill and John Ed—have a plan to reenter the industry with a one-barrel-a-day micro-distillery using equipment they salvaged from Michter's years ago. Although the American whiskey industry is much smaller than it was even a generation ago, the Beams are still a large part of it. As long as whiskey is made in America, somewhere somehow a Beam probably will be making it.

Chapter Thirteen

Two Sides of the Whiskey Question.

Whiskey has been known to bring out the worst in people, but also the best, and sometimes both at the same time. Noah S. 'Soggie' Sweat Jr. of Mississippi was a judge and law school professor who before ascending to the bench served one term in the state legislature, from 1948 to 1952. He is remembered today primarily for two achievements. In 1970, he founded the Mississippi Judicial College at the University of Mississippi, the first institution in that state for the formal education of judges, judicial clerks, administrators, and court reporters. He is in this book, however, for an earlier accomplishment, a wonderful speech he wrote and delivered to the Mississippi legislature in 1952. Poor Mississippi was the last state to lift Prohibition. Relief did not officially come until 1966, but the reality before then was a monument to political duplicity and hypocrisy. Throughout the state, bars and package stores operated illegally but openly. The state somehow even collected a 'black market tax' on the illicit liquor sales, yet any elected official who proposed a sensible reform of the system was committing political suicide. Sweat's speech, therefore, was a comic masterpiece with a serious purpose. He was just 28 years old when he wrote and delivered it. The speech went like this:

"I had not intended to discuss this controversial subject at this particular time. However, I want you to know that I do not shun controversy. On the contrary, I will take a stand on any issue at any time, regardless of how fraught with controversy it might be. You have asked me how I feel about whiskey. All right, here is how I feel about whiskey.

"If when you say whiskey, you mean the devil's brew, the poison scourge, the bloody monster that defiles innocence, dethrones reason, destroys the home, creates misery and poverty, yea, literally takes the bread from the mouths of little children; if you mean the evil drink that topples the Christian man and woman from the pinnacle of righteous, gracious living into the bottomless pit of degradation and despair and shame and helplessness and hopelessness—then certainly I am against it.

"But if, when you say whiskey, you mean the oil of conversation, the philosophic wine, the ale that is consumed when good fellows get together, that puts a song in their hearts and laughter on their lips and the warm glow of contentment in their eyes; if you mean Christmas cheer; if you mean the stimulating drink that puts the spring in the old gentleman's step on a frosty, crispy morning; if you mean the drink which enables a man to magnify his joy and his happiness and to forget, if only for a little while, life's great tragedies and heartaches and sorrows; if you mean that drink the sale of which pours into our treasuries untold millions of dollars which are used to provide tender care for our little crippled children, our blind, our deaf, our pitiful aged and infirm, to build highways and hospitals and schools, then certainly I am for it.

"This is my stand, and I will not compromise."

Chapter Fourteen

Fall from Grace; the History of Old Crow.

Foods and beverages can be a way of experiencing history. By eating and drinking the same foods our ancestors did, we can recreate and experience in a small way an important aspect of their daily lives. Like historic recipes made at home using traditional ingredients and techniques, unchanged commercial products can also provide a window into an earlier time.

Despite a few changes in technology, modern bourbon whiskey is a product 19th century drinkers would still recognize, but many of America's historically great whiskies have been lost through industry consolidation. Mark Brown, President and CEO of Buffalo Trace Distillery, estimates that 50 to 60 historic bourbon recipes have disappeared. Even before the 1970s crash in bourbon sales occurred, the great rye whiskey industries of Pennsylvania,

Maryland and Virginia had followed the once great rum industry of New England into oblivion. Ohio, Indiana, Illinois, Kansas and Missouri also had thriving distilling industries at one time. Illinois once rivaled Kentucky as a whiskey maker, but today its distilleries make only GNS, mostly for fuel and industrial uses. Today, the entire American whiskey industry consists of a dozen or so distilleries concentrated in Kentucky and Tennessee.

Among America's once great whiskies, none has fallen further than Old Crow. There is still a whiskey sold under the Old Crow name and it is an authentic Kentucky Straight Bourbon Whiskey, just as its label says. Yet despite those facts, Old Crow is the premier example of an American 'lost whiskey.'

The Old Crow brand originated with Dr. James C. Crow, who is credited with developing the sour mash process while working as a distiller at the Old Oscar Pepper Distillery in Woodford County. Crow was born in Scotland in 1789 and emigrated to Kentucky by way of Pennsylvania in the 1820s. He worked as a distiller for Colonel Willis Field on Grier's Creek and for Zachariah Henry on Glenn's Creek, both also in Woodford County, before going to work for Pepper in 1838. While working for Pepper he also sometimes worked at the Old Anderson Johnson Distillery nearby.

Crow was trained in Edinburgh as a physician and chemist, so he knew more about the science of distilling than most of his contemporaries. His sour mash process tempered each batch of new mash with spent beer from the previous distillation. He was also a stickler for hygiene. Both of these practices kept the fermenting mash from being tainted by bacteria, wild yeast, and other microorganisms, assuring consistent quality from batch to batch. This innovation revolutionized American whiskey making. As Crow experimented and gained experience, he formed other strong opinions about how quality whiskey should be made. He insisted that no more than two and one-half gallons of unadulterated whiskey could be made from a bushel of grain. He also was reputed to be the first distiller to sell only aged whiskey. Before Crow, distillers primarily sold 'common whiskey,' the un-aged spirit. A shrewd businessman, Oscar Pepper demanded and received the premium price of 25 cents a gallon for Dr. Crow's increasingly popular product, at a time when 15 cents was the going rate.

Although Crow worked primarily as a distiller he also practiced medicine, mostly without charge. In his leisure time he was fond of reciting the poems of Robert Burns. He liked to hunt and was a crack shot. His whiskey had many famous admirers and he socialized with some of them, including fellow Kentuckians Henry Clay and John Crittenden. He was considered to be a man of intellect and refinement. Other prominent men of the day who may not have known Dr. Crow personally but who praised his whiskey included Andrew Jackson, General U. S. Grant, Daniel Webster and William Henry Harrison.

The reputation of Crow whiskey spread far and wide. Two letters written in 1849 by Robert Letcher, a Kentucky politician, indicate that it was famous for its quality and rich, amber color by that early date. The reference in Letcher's letters to the red hue of Crow's whiskey is the first historical evidence we have of American whiskey being aged in new, charred oak barrels. Letcher was writing to a friend, Orlando Brown, the United States Commissioner for Indian Affairs, who had complained to Letcher about some vague malaise. As a cure, Letcher sent him a supply of Old Crow bourbon, preceded by a note in which he described Old Crow as the "Red Cretur."

James Crow died suddenly, at work, in 1856. He was buried in the Versailles Cemetery. His wife and only child, a daughter, died soon thereafter and are buried beside him. His mantle was passed to his employer, Oscar Pepper, and to one of his assistants, William Mitchell. When Pepper died a few years later a consortium of investors led by E. H. Taylor Jr., who was legal guardian to Pepper's young son, James, purchased from the Pepper estate all rights to the Old Crow name along with the remaining inventory of Crow-made whiskey. The new owners hired Mitchell as their distiller. He later imparted Crow's recipe and methods to his successor, Van Johnson, who passed them on to his son, Leo, so the chain of continuity from Crow's day well into the 20th century is strong.

At some point during Van Johnson's tenure, the exact date being unknown but probably near the turn of the century, Johnson wrote out the recipe in detail— under the heading 'James Crow's Formula for Making Whiskey'—and gave it to a prominent local attorney, Thomas Noble Lindsey, for safekeeping.

There is nothing particularly unusual or distinctive about this recipe, but it illustrates how bourbon was made a century ago. It reads as follows:

> Use in 100 bushels of bourbon mash, 12 to 15% of barley malt, ground, 8 to 10% of rye, ground, and 75 to 80% of corn, ground.

In starting up the distillery and using small tubs, put say 80 lbs. of corn meal in the tub and cook with say 30 to 40 gallons of boiling water. Let set for 4 to 5 hours, then stir and cool to 150 degrees to 160 degrees Fahrenheit and then add rye, say 8 to 10 lbs. Then cool down by stirring to 135-148 and then add malt, say 12 to 15 lbs. Then cool down to 115 degrees Fahrenheit and add cold water enough to bring it down to 68-78 according to the temperature of the weather. Then fill the fermenter with water at same setting temperature, then add yeast which has been made say 1½ to 3½ lbs. to the bushel.

Continue the above for four days and thereafter cook the corn meal with boiling slop, then let stand from 12 to 24 hours, then break up and cool by stirring to 122-160. Then add rye, same percent as above, and cool to 120-130. Then add malt and hold for two hours. Then break up, run to fermenters and fill according to the weather, and add either fresh yeast, or yeast taken from the previous tubs. The tubs for the first three days of the week are set at say 72-78 and the last three days say 66-72.

Then run the beer into the stills, copper preferred and boil until the spirit is practically exhausted. Then run this spirit obtained from first distillation, and which is held in tubs for the purpose, into the copper doubler and there boil until the whiskey so made would show above proof in the receiving room. The remainder being boiled until the whiskey is practically exhausted and which after cutting off is run into the low wine tub and distilled over again.

YEAST. Use proper proportions of rye, say 1½ lbs. to the bushel, and cook same in 15 to 20 gallons of water to a temperature of say 160 to 175 for say 10 to 20 minutes; then follow with barley malt, same percent, and let stand 24 hours at least to sour and cool to 70-76 degrees. Then stock it with jug yeast previously prepared.

In about 1878 the original Pepper plant was sold and a new Old Crow Distillery was built on property along the same road, also adjacent to Glenn's Creek, but much nearer to Frankfort, almost to where Glenn's Creek joins the Kentucky River. Whiskey was made there according to Dr. Crow's recipe until Prohibition and was resumed there after repeal. Under new owners National Distillers, new boilers were installed, along with a new beer still and doubler, nine new fermenters, three new high wine tanks and two new cistern room tanks. A quadruple effect evaporator formerly used at a distillery in Cincinnati was also installed. (Evaporators are used to dry spent beer so it can be sold as animal feed.) During World War II, major changes were made to the distillery's equipment so it could produce 190+ proof alcohol for war use. After the war, whiskey-making resumed and Old Crow became one of the world's top selling bourbons. Until 1952, it was sold only as a bond, i.e., 100 proof. In that year, an 86 proof version was introduced.

In the 1960s, with sales still booming, production capacity at the Old Crow plant was increased significantly. According to a former National Distillers employee who was the last master distiller at Crow before it was acquired by Jim Beam in 1987, it was during this expansion that the original formula was accidentally changed. The error was in the percentage of backset returned to the new mash. This is ironic because the use of backset to condition new mash is the very essence of the sour mash process introduced by Dr. Crow. Despite falling sales, many customer complaints about the product's new flavor, and even negative reviews from the distillery's own tasting panels, the plant's managers were either unwilling or unable to correct the mistake until just a few years before Jim Beam closed the plant in 1987. But by then the damage had been done.

Sales of almost all bourbon brands declined during the 1970s and 1980s, but none worse than Old Crow. In addition to losing sales, it also lost market share. Formerly number one, today it does not even rank in the top ten. For most of the period between Prohibition and Old Crow's fall from grace, the brand's chief rival for the position of best-selling bourbon was Jim Beam. As a final irony, the Old Crow whiskey in stores today *is* Jim Beam. That is, it is whiskey made by Jim Beam from the standard Jim Beam bourbon mash bill. The other major bourbon brand Jim Beam acquired from National was Old Grand-Dad. That product is still made using its original yeast and mash bill. Old Crow is not. Jim Beam sells Old Crow as a bottom shelf 'value' brand. It is not very good, nor is it the same Old Crow produced by Dr. Crow and enjoyed by Daniel Webster and other famous fans. That whiskey is long gone, lost in the mists of time.

In addition to the brand itself, there are a few other remaining legacies of Old Crow. The original Old Crow Distillery, where Crow and Pepper made whiskey history, is today's Woodford Reserve. The plant is located on Glenn's Creek Road in Woodford County, between Versailles and Frankfort. It was restored by current owner Brown-Forman in 1996 and is open for public tours. The old limestone buildings are essentially as they were when rebuilt by E. H. Taylor in 1867. Leaving Woodford Reserve, if you continue on Glenn's Creek Road toward Frankfort you will come to the second Old Crow Distillery, the one built in 1878 that operated until 1987. It is not open to the public but most of it can be seen from the road. Much of this facility is now in ruins, although most of the rackhouses are still in use. It is right next door to the plant E. H. Taylor built for himself, Old Taylor, which is the name of another once-proud bourbon now made by Jim Beam as a shadow of its former self.

In Frankfort, on Louisville Road, is a restored Georgian Revival stone mansion built in 1900 with profits from the Old Crow distillery. It is called Berry Hill and is owned by the Commonwealth of Kentucky. It houses some state offices but the first floor is open to the public and contains period furnishings. Its most notable feature is an elaborate music room built in the Gothic Revival style that includes a full-size cathedral organ. The mansion's original owner was George F. Berry, who was vice-president of W. A. Gaines and Co., the corporation that owned Old Crow between 1887 and Prohibition. (E. H. Taylor had sold his interest in 1870.) George Berry's father, Hiram, was one of the original investors recruited by Taylor twenty years before. Although Berry's title was vice-president, the corporation's chief executive was based in New York, so Berry was the principal local boss. The W. A. Gaines name also lives on as the assumed business name under which Jim Beam makes and markets its Old Crow bourbon today.

Chapter Fifteen

The Elephant in the Room.

When whiskey marketers, whiskey writers and whiskey drinkers talk about 'bourbon this' and 'bourbon that,' they ignore, sometimes deliberately, the elephant in the room. Such as when a producer says their product is 'the best-selling bourbon.' True, to most people, bourbon is synonymous with American whiskey. It is the name—and this part *is* true—of America's principal whiskey style, and yet the #1 best selling American whiskey does not have the word 'bourbon' on its label. That product is Jack Daniel's Tennessee whiskey.

Though not a bourbon, Jack Daniel's is a pillar of the bourbon industry and unlike straight rye, America's other major non-bourbon straight whiskey style, Jack Daniel's whiskey is a bourbon in every tangible sense. It looks, smells and tastes like a bourbon, and is made the same way. One could even argue that Jack Daniel's embodies the bourbon type due to its great popularity, yet always with the caveat that it is not technically bourbon. The only part of the Jack Daniel's production process that differs from how bourbon is made is the famous 'Lincoln County Process.' For that process a column approximately ten feet high is packed with sugar maple charcoal. New whiskey, straight from the stills, is run through this filtration system before it is barreled. This type of filtration is an old rectification technique commonly practiced during the 19th century in both the United States and Canada. The effect is similar to what happens in the barrel when whiskey interfaces with the char. As such, it can be thought of as jump-starting the aging process.

Jack Daniel's is a rarity among long-standing whiskey brands for another reason. It has been sold only once in its long history. Jack Daniel started the company in 1866 and turned it over to his sister's son, Lem Motlow, and a cousin, Dick Daniel. Motlow bought Daniel out and eventually passed the company on to his sons Reagor, Robert, Daniel and Clifford. They sold it to Brown-Forman in 1956. Daniel's has also been very stable in the whiskey-making end of the business. Jimmy Bedford, current master distiller, is only the fifth person to hold that job since Jack Daniel himself. Jack Daniel's is also unique in being the flagship product of Brown-Forman. No other large, public company stakes more of its corporate fate on the success of an American straight whiskey.

The marketing for Jack Daniel's has always walked a fine line, trying to look small when it is really huge. The secret has been to tie everything back to tiny Lynchburg—a 'company town' if ever there was one—and to Mister Jack himself. The whiskey, the man, the town and the legend are all of one piece. Lynchburg is the original distillery-as-tourist-destination. Although no one does it like Jack, almost all of the whiskey distilleries in America now offer something for tourists. Another principle of the brand's success, violated in recent years, was to stay away from line extensions. Until the introduction of Gentleman Jack in the 1990s there were just two labels, the ubiquitous black and the lesser known green. Now there is a single barrel and a line of pre-mixed cocktails, not to mention mustard, barbecue sauce and a million other licensed products. A 'flavored malt beverage' called Jack Daniel's Original Hard Cola, made by Miller Brewing, was introduced in 2002 but seems to be foundering. So far the brand does not seem to be suffering from overexposure. It just keeps getting bigger.

The folks who market Jack Daniel's never miss a trick. In 1999, when the brand celebrated the 150th anniversary of Jack's birth (three years late, but who cares) one of their promotions was called 'Crack Jack's Safe.' The reference was to a large office safe he owned and supposedly kicked in 1905, injuring his toe leading to its amputation and, eventually, his death in 1911. Is this a fun brand, or what?

The Jack Daniel's story is full of ironies like that. Famously, it is made in a dry county. Although Tennessee law now permits bottles of Jack to be sold in the gift shop, the saloon serves nothing stronger than lemonade. Jack Daniel's takes pride in its Tennessee roots, but is owned by a Kentucky corporation. It cultivates the image of a small and unsophisticated operation when it is actually huge and worldly. The greatest irony, of course, is that this defiantly non-bourbon whiskey defines so much of what bourbon is supposed to be.

Although it all goes back to Jack, before there was Jack Daniel there was Dan Call, a kindly farmer-distiller who took in young Jack when the boy ran away from home. It is an old and sad but familiar tale, complete with a wicked stepmother, like something that might have made a good 1950s Walt Disney film, except they would have made him a tanner or something other than a whiskey distiller. Jack was a small and unattractive child, a 'runt' by some accounts, whose mother died shortly after he was born. His father soon remarried and Jack's stepmother was not sufficiently nurturing so he turned to Call, a young man who recently had inherited a farm in the area. Call had a whiskey still but he also had a congregation. In addition to farming and whiskey-making he was a country preacher, and his flock didn't care for the whiskey-making part of his operation, so he sold his still to Jack, just 14 years old at the time. Jack proceeded to make whiskey and sell it successfully around the neighborhood. I envision something like the lemonade stands we all had as kids.

By 1866, Jack was a prosperous 20-year-old entrepreneur. That year he bought some land over by Lynchburg, in Lincoln County, Tennessee, at the exact location where the famed 'Lincoln County Process' is supposed to have originated. (County boundaries subsequently changed and Lynchburg is now in Moore County.) Although charcoal rectification is hardly peculiar to Tennessee, the exclusive use of sugar maple for the charcoal does seem to be a unique feature of the Tennessee practice.

Instinctively and before there was even a name for it, Jack Daniel understood brand marketing and made himself into the personification of his product. Much like Kentuckian Harlan 'Colonel' Sanders in the 1950s, Jack decided he should look the part of a Southern gentleman distillery owner from an earlier era. He wore a wide-brimmed planter's hat, a long frock coat, a colorful vest and a string tie, along with a carefully trimmed goatee. His unusually small stature (5'5" and 120 pounds) made him stand out even more.

Jack's nephew, Lem Motlow, joined the company in the 1880s and soon was running it. He took over after Jack's death and later his four sons joined him in the business. Prohibition in Tennessee came early and stayed late. The state shut down all of its distilleries in 1911, but the Motlows simply moved to St. Louis, then to Alabama when the St. Louis plant burned down. Like everyone else they were out of business during National Prohibition, and because of Tennessee's reluctance they were one of the last companies to restart afterwards. Tennessee finally repealed state prohibition in 1938 after Lem got himself elected to the state legislature.

By the 1950s, the Motlow brothers faced the same capital problems confronted by many family-owned distilleries after Prohibition. In 1956, Brown-Forman bought the company but left the Motlows in charge, placing Reagor Motlow on the Brown-Forman board. Today the Motlows are gone from senior management and the Daniel's operation is much less autonomous than it once was, but that is because in many ways the tail now wags the dog. Jack Daniel's Tennessee whiskey is the flagship of Brown-Forman's fleet, accounting for about half of the company's profits. The Brown-Forman portfolio also includes Early Times Kentucky whisky (also not bourbon, due to the reuse of some cooperage), Old Forester bourbon (the founding brand and former flagship), Woodford Reserve bourbon, Southern Comfort (an imitation whiskey, technically a liqueur), Canadian Mist Canadian whiskey, several prominent single malts (Glenmorangie, Glen Moray, Ardbeg), Appleton rum, several wine brands (Korbel, Fetzer, Bolla), and prestigious durables lines like Lenox china and crystal, Dansk and Gorham tableware, and Hartmann luggage.

Jack Daniel's calls itself 'Tennessee Sour Mash Whiskey.' Legally, that term is unlike the term 'Kentucky Straight Bourbon Whiskey' in several respects. The words 'straight' and 'bourbon' have specific legal meanings in the Code of Federal Regulations (CFR), as does 'whiskey.' The words 'sour mash' do not. Nor do the state names appear in the CFR, although their use is regulated by state law. Although the term 'Tennessee whiskey' does not appear in the CFR, Reagor Motlow in 1941 solicited and received a letter from the Alcohol Tax Unit of the Treasury Department acknowledging that Tennessee whiskey is distinct from bourbon. Recently, international treaties have recognized Tennessee whiskey as a distinctive product of the United States.

Jack Daniel's is not the only Tennessee whiskey. The other one is George Dickel, also made in south-central Tennessee, a few miles from Lynchburg in Tullahoma. Though a significant international brand by most standards, Dickel is a pipsqueak compared to

Daniel's and not important enough to parent Diageo to be listed on the company's web site as one of its products. When Diageo abandoned the American whiskey business in 1999, it retained only two American whiskey brands, Dickel and I. W. Harper bourbon. Although it kept selling Dickel, it stopped making and marketing it. In the Fall of 2002, marketing resumed but when fans of the whiskey asked longtime Dickel master distiller Dave Backus when he was going to start distilling again, he cryptically answered, "if you drink it all, we'll make more." Apparently they drank enough, because Dickel started to make whiskey again, with much fanfare, in September of 2003. They market two expressions, a white label and a black, and although neither carries an age statement, the white is more expensive and presumed to be older whiskey. Like Jack Daniel's, Dickel sends all of its new whiskey through a big stack of sugar maple charcoal before it goes into the barrels. Dickel's method is slightly different in that they chill the whiskey first.

The brand's namesake, George A. Dickel, was a real person but not a distiller. He was born in Darmstadt, Germany, about 1818 and around 1853 he came to Tennessee and established a wholesale whiskey business in Nashville. He also operated a retail liquor store there. In 1888, George A. Dickel and Co. acquired the sole rights to bottle and distribute all of the whiskey produced by the Cascade Distillery, which had been established in 1877 in Coffee County, Tennessee, and was by then two-thirds owned by Dickel's partner and brother-in-law, Victor Schwab. A contract obligating a wholesaler to buy all the production of a distillery, provided the distillery renounces all other customers, was common in those days. Distillers made whiskey, wholesalers sold it to retailers, and retailers sold it to consumers, a three-tier distribution system much like the one we have today. Except in those days the wholesalers, not the producers, owned the brands. Because distillers were perennially short of capital, many wholesalers also wound up owning the distilleries. That was how the Dickel company came to own Cascade.

Although 1888 linked the Dickel company and Cascade together for all time, it was otherwise a bad year for George. Seventy years old and in failing health, he was injured in a fall from a horse. The accident forced his retirement and he died six years later. In 1889, Schwab acquired sole ownership of Cascade upon the death of his partner, Maclin Davis. After Dickel's death the Schwab family and George's widow—Augusta, 20 years his junior—ran both companies until Tennessee Prohibition closed the distillery in 1911. They then had whiskey made for them in Kentucky until National Prohibition shut everyone down. One of the Kentucky distilleries that made Cascade whiskey was A. Ph. Stitzel. After Prohibition ended, the successor company, Stitzel-Weller, advertised Cascade Hollow whiskey as one of its brands. The Schwabs sold the Dickel name to Schenley, which made a George Dickel bourbon at the Frankfort distillery that is now Buffalo Trace. Schenley got back the rights to the Cascade name and in 1958 a veteran Schenley distiller named Ralph Dupps was assigned to build a new distillery near where the old one had been at Cascade Hollow.

The charcoal filtering process used by both Tennessee whiskies tends to give them a much milder flavor than most standard (i.e., four to six year old) bourbons, which makes the Tennesseans easier to drink. They possess that ineffable (and much overrated) quality known as smoothness. Dickel has even fewer rough edges than Daniel's. Some of Kentucky's distilleries achieve a similar result through high distillation proof and a mash bill light on flavor grain. All three methods are effective at eliminating some of the more objectionable congeners.

Although there are only two producers of Tennessee whiskey, both are significant participants in the drinks category that includes bourbon, whatever you choose to call it. Technically, the American whiskey category has two segments, straights and blends, but Tennessee whiskey is neither according to the regulations, although it is more like a straight. Kentucky whiskey (e.g., Early Times) is similarly homeless. I consider both types straight whiskey as do most liquor distributors and retailers. Most important of all, consumers are unbothered by the distinction, even though some big bourbon producers from time to time will make dark references to non-bourbons as if they are some kind of plague. It's a little confusing, but not terribly so. Everyone needs to get over it.

Chapter Sixteen

Something About Some Roses.

Here in the U.S., Four Roses is dimly remembered as an undistinguished American blended whiskey, something your grandfather may have drunk if he was cheap and not too particular. But in Europe and other overseas markets, Four Roses is a bourbon—a good one—and one of the leaders in bourbon's growing international popularity. It is the top bourbon in Japan, France, Spain, The Netherlands and Italy.

Four Roses was, for a long time, a product of the Seagram Company. When Seagrams was broken-up in 2000 after its sale to France's Vivendi, Four Roses and the distillery that makes it were acquired by Kirin Brewery of Japan, which had long been partners with Seagrams in the Japanese spirits business. Back when Seagrams was still the owner, the man who runs the Four Roses plant—master distiller Jim Rutledge—persuaded the company to let Four Roses bourbon be sold in a few retail outlets in Kentucky and Indiana, so at least the people who make it could buy it. Since

Kirin has taken over, distribution has widened but it is still mostly sold in Kentucky and only the standard, 80 proof, yellow label expression is available even there. Overseas there are premium and single barrel versions.

Standard Four Roses yellow label is a worthy bourbon and an unusual one, unlike any other on the market. It uses a production method that is characteristic of the Seagrams philosophy of combining different whiskies to create and maintain a consistently pleasing flavor profile. Sam Bronfman, who built Seagrams into the world's biggest liquor company, always believed this was the best way to make whiskey and Jim Rutledge, who worked for Seagrams for 35 years, agrees. Because of its production method, one might reasonably say that Four Roses is a *blend* of different bourbons. This would be true as the word is ordinarily used, but 'blend' is a loaded term in the American whiskey business. Four Roses bourbon is a *bourbon*, not a blended whiskey like Seagram's Seven Crown, because it is a mixture of straight bourbons and nothing else.

To create the particular mixture that is Four Roses yellow label, they start with ten different bourbons. To arrive at ten whiskies they match two different mash bills with each of five different proprietary yeasts. The mash bills differ in the ratio of corn to rye. One of the two would be considered a standard bourbon while the other would be considered a high rye bourbon, similar to Old Grand-Dad. They also mix in a few different distillation years so in the end they use 14 different whiskies to hit the desired flavor target. Although they don't put an age statement on it,

Rutledge says the youngest whiskey in the mix is about
5½ years old and the oldest is about 10.

Four Roses has a long history and was one of the
earliest bourbon brands. For a long time on both sides
of Prohibition it was a product of the Paul Jones
Company. Jones had been a colonel in the
Confederate Army. After the war, he and his son
established a distillery in Atlanta, Georgia. Their initial
brand was called Paul Jones Whiskey. They
subsequently relocated to Tennessee where they got
out of distilling but brokered and sold whiskey made
by others. In 1886 they moved to Louisville, Kentucky.
Two years later they acquired some assets from the
Rose family of Tennessee, including the Four Roses
brand name. The Jones company at various times in its
advertising told two different stories about how the
Four Roses name originated. In one, the four roses
commemorate Mr. Rose's four daughters. In later
years, probably to get the Rose family out of the
picture, they devised a tale in which a corsage of four
roses is worn by a young lady to indicate her
acceptance of a marriage proposal from Mr. Jones.

So although Rose was originally a family name,
today it is all about the flowers. Some of the people
responsible for marketing the brand worry that the
flowers make the brand seem too feminine. They may
be right, but roses also are an important part of
Kentucky heritage in a way that is gender-neutral. The
Kentucky Derby has long been called 'the run for the
roses' because the winning horse is draped with a
blanket of them immediately after the race, and roses
are a key part of Derby imagery. Although Four Roses
has never tied itself to the Derby, the point is that roses

in a Kentucky heritage context aren't necessarily girly. Considering the brand's long absence from the U.S. market, flowers are the least of its problems. For most American consumers it is essentially a new brand.

But back to our story. By 1902, the American whiskey industry was consolidating and the Paul Jones Company combined with several other firms to form the Frankfort Distillery, Inc. Frankfort, which was based near the city of that name, was headed for a time by Lawrence Jones Jr., Paul's grandson. During Prohibition they operated a consolidation warehouse at the site on Elkhorn Creek that became Old Grand-Dad after Prohibition, and which Jim Beam owns today and uses for aging and bottling. The Frankfort Distillery was one of a small group of companies licensed to sell medicinal whiskey during Prohibition. At one point they produced one-quarter of the nation's medicinal whiskey supply. When Prohibition ended, Frankfort's warehouses were empty and the plant was in ruins, so the company sold that property, built a new distillery in Louisville and gave it the Frankfort name. In Louisville, though, most people just called it Four Roses, as that was the principal product made there. Roy Beam was master distiller, with help from his father, Joseph L. Beam, a couple of his brothers, and two of his sons. One of Roy Beam's sons, Charlie, eventually wound up at the current Four Roses facility in Lawrenceburg, Kentucky, where he was master distiller until he retired in 1982.

In 1928, Samuel Bronfman—from his vantage point in Canada—became convinced that America's experiment with national Prohibition would be abandoned eventually. He prepared for that day and when it did end he quickly bought a distillery property in Lawrenceburg, Indiana, which Seagrams owned until its recent demise. When World War II came, Seagrams went on a buying spree, acquiring another dozen or so Kentucky distilleries, including Frankfort. They used them to make alcohol for the war effort. Lawrence Jones died in 1941, ending that family's involvement in this story. When the war ended, Seagrams closed Frankfort and transferred the Four Roses name to a distillery they had purchased in Lawrenceburg, Kentucky, where the name remains to this day. The fact that for many years the two main U.S. distilleries owned by Seagrams were both in towns named Lawrenceburg was pure coincidence, but a source of constant confusion.

After Charlie Beam retired from Four Roses in 1982, Ova Haney moved from the Indiana Lawrenceburg to the Kentucky one as master distiller. He was succeeded by Jim Rutledge in 1998. Unlike some distillers and some distillery companies, Beam, Haney and now Rutledge have always been willing to talk frankly and in detail about the way they make their whiskey. In addition to the bourbons they make there, the plant still provides straight whiskey for Seagrams Seven Crown and other Diageo blended whiskey products. They also make Bulleit bourbon, a Diageo product. The title once held by Seagrams, of world's largest drinks company, is now held by Diageo, but Diageo owns no Kentucky distilleries.

Starting with their formula, everything about Four Roses is a little bit unusual. The distillery is built in a Spanish Mission style and its aging houses, instead of being close to the distillery like most, are 40 miles away, outside of Bardstown at a place called Lotus. There are several traditional-style rackhouses right across the road from the Four Roses distillery but they are owned by Lawrenceburg's other distillery, Wild Turkey. The buildings where Four Roses is aged at Lotus are single story structures sometimes called 'flathouses.' This type of building is believed to provide more uniform aging and certainly makes it easier to get barrels in and out. Every day, green whiskey from the distillery is shipped in tank trucks to Lotus, where it is barreled and placed in storage. Lotus now has a gift shop and welcomes visitors.

Even though the distillery in Lawrenceburg has been called Four Roses for 60 years, some old timers still call it Old Prentice or Old Joe. A distillery has stood on or near that site for almost 200 years. The first was on Gilbert's Creek, a few dozen yards from the current plant. It was known as the Old Joe Distillery and was started in 1818 by 'Old Joe' Payton, an early settler. Legend has it that as soon as Payton acquired the land he pitched a tent and set up his stills. Erecting a house was a lower priority than making a batch of whiskey. Ownership of the Old Joe plant passed to the Hawkins family in 1840. In 1855, the Hawkins built a second distillery around the corner from Old Joe on the present Four Roses site. They named their new distillery Old Prentice. In 1857 they sold Old Joe to Medley S. Bond. After the Civil War, T. B. Ripy, one of the most important Anderson County distillers, bought Old Joe and then quickly resold it to Captain Wiley Searcy, a distinguished Civil War veteran, who shortly sold it back to the Hawkins family. In 1904, the Hawkins sold the Old Prentice plant to the five sons of

John Thompson Street Brown (better known as J. T. S. Brown). J. T. S. Brown was the half-brother and partner of Brown-Forman founder George Garvin Brown. Like their cousins at Brown-Forman in Louisville, Graham, Davis, Creel, J. T. S. Jr., and Hewitt were all distillers. Their two principal brands were Old Prentice and J. T. S. Brown, both bourbons.

In 1909, the original Old Joe distillery was destroyed by fire and the Hawkins family sold it back to the Ripy brothers, who rebuilt it. In 1912, the Hawkins bought it back. Meanwhile, in 1910, the Browns tore down the facility at Old Prentice and built the present Spanish Mission-style building. They operated there until Prohibition began. While the distillery was dark, most of its equipment was sold. After repeal, ownership of the two neighboring plants gets even more confusing, but it appears that the Hawkins threw in with the Browns to refurbish Old Prentice, resuming production there in 1934 at 400 bushels per day, under the leadership of Creel Brown Jr. The Hawkins family brought with them the Old Joe name. Around the corner, the original Old Joe plant was acquired by a Cincinnati whiskey merchant named Sam Friedman, who operated it under the name Bonds Mill. At some point it was purchased by Schenley, one of the industry giants at that time. Old Prentice/J. T. S. Brown remained independent until World War II started, then it quickly passed through several owners until it was acquired by Seagrams and renamed Four Roses. Seagrams increased its capacity to the present 2,400 bushels per day. The Old Joe and Old Prentice brand names were discontinued and the J. T. S. Brown name was sold to Heaven Hill.

After the war, Seagrams began closing plants until all that remained were the two Lawrenceburgs. Eventually, probably in the 1960s, the original Old Joe plant on Gilbert's Creek also closed for good.

Today both the staff at Four Roses and the community of American whiskey fans are hopeful that this distillery will blossom (pardon the pun) under Kirin's ownership. We especially are looking forward to the U.S. introduction of the premium and single barrel expressions. Don't worry about the name or the pretty flowers on the label. Just give us the whiskey.

Chapter Seventeen

How to Taste American Straight Whiskey.

Careful tasting is an important part of the way American straight whiskey is made. Critical tasting can also be a fun part of the whiskey experience for drinkers, but some people find it intimidating. "I don't taste any raisins," they moan. When professional tasters wax eloquently about "red berry fruits," "perfumed hickory" and "emphatic mint toffee," the bar gets raised further still. Many ordinary drinkers conclude that the ability to taste critically is a special gift reserved for individuals born with an unusually sensitive palate, an unusually vivid imagination, or both.

In fact, anyone with normal sense organs and sufficient interest can learn how to taste whiskey critically. Like most skills, it primarily requires practice. Whiskey tasting is much like wine tasting and a similar vocabulary is used. Published professionals like to expand that vocabulary using creative writing techniques. If they sometimes appear to be showing off, it is that creative writing muscle they are flexing and not some kind of super sensitive palate.

At a distillery, professional tasters serve several different functions. Before barrels are dumped for bottling, a sample from each is carefully nosed. This is a final quality check to make sure nothing has contaminated the whiskey over the long years of aging. The taster extracts a small sample, dilutes it with an equal volume of water, and smells it to detect any taint that would cause the whiskey to be rejected. This taster does not evaluate the whiskey beyond an accept/reject determination. Such a check must be done at this stage because the contents of multiple barrels will be mixed together in a large tank prior to bottling and one bad barrel could spoil the whole bunch. Dilution of the whiskey sample with water is necessary to protect the taster's olfactory bulb. American whiskey comes out of its barrel at somewhere between 110 and 140 proof. Undiluted, the whiskey would quickly numb the taster's olfactory nerve cells. Too much exposure to undiluted barrel-proof whiskey could even cause permanent damage. A distillery will employ several tasters for this job and limit the number of barrels each can sample during a given work shift.

A more comprehensive tasting takes place after a batch of barrels has been dumped. At this point, the distillery's tasting panel is convened. The tasting panel always includes the master distiller along with other employees of the facility. The tasters don't necessarily all work in the distillery part of the operation and tasting is not their sole or even primary job. They might be warehouse workers, or bottling line mechanics, or marketing managers, or even retirees. On the tasting panel, their charge is to taste the just-dumped batch of whiskey and compare it to reference samples of past batches of that particular product. Every whiskey has a taste profile determined at the time of that product's creation by the master distiller and other company decision-makers. The exact way that particular whiskey should taste is enshrined in a reference sample, i.e., a bottle of whiskey labeled and stored away for that purpose. The tasting panel must decide if the current batch is a close enough match to the standard to be bottled as that product. If not, more whiskey may be added to the batch to bring it closer to the standard. If the whiskey tastes too green, older whiskey will be added. If it tastes too old, younger whiskey will go into the mixture. If, for some reason, the previous profile cannot be matched or can be matched only in a limited quantity, then the distillery may choose to limit availability of that particular product. This process of selecting and mixing whiskies to match a taste target is how two different products, made at the same distillery using the same basic mash bill and yeast can taste distinctly different from each other and yet remain consistently true to their own taste profile for decades.

The third role professional tasting plays at a distillery is in regular sampling of the whiskey as it ages. Samples are periodically extracted from barrels and tested (i.e., tasted) to evaluate their progress. This is primarily the responsibility of the master distiller, but others may also be pressed into service.

The fourth role is in the creation of new products. Again, this is primarily the master distiller's job, but sales and marketing, and senior company management may also be involved. Members of the public may even be recruited in the formative stages of a new product. The new product might be created from scratch, with a unique mash bill and yeast, and other methodologies employed to realize a particular desired outcome. More often, a new product is created by searching the rackhouses for batches of whiskey that exhibit certain characteristics, starting with an age target or a desired proof or some other baseline characteristic from which the new product can be built. Several prototype samples might be created and compared before a final profile is selected. This then becomes the standard for that product against which all future batches will be judged.

Unless you work at or are planning to start a distillery, you probably won't need any of those particular skills, but you can still learn how to taste critically for your own enjoyment. Before we discuss *how* to taste, let's consider *what* to taste. But before we do that, a word about *how many* to taste.

As mentioned earlier, tasting spirits can strain the organs of taste and smell. To critically taste a selection of whiskies, five or six different selections at a sitting is about the limit and three or four is probably better. This can be a hard rule to accept, especially in a social situation where everyone wants you to taste their favorite. Cleansing your palate regularly with room temperature water and bread or unsalted crackers will help, but realistically your senses are compromised after five or six selections, and that's not even considering the effects of intoxication. You can deal with that by tasting and then discarding your sample, expectoration is a well established practice in wine tasting circles. However, that only prevents intoxication. It doesn't spare your taste and smell organs. The suggestions below assume that each suggested tasting suite will encompass one tasting session.

If you go to a whiskey tasting at a bar, restaurant or package store it probably will be run or sponsored by a producer or distributor and cover the range of that company's product line, or some subset thereof. There is nothing wrong with that kind of tasting, and it certainly serves the marketer's promotional purposes, but if you want to mount a tasting of your own, either just for yourself or for a group of friends, there are much more interesting ways to go about it. Here are some suggestions for different suites of American whiskey to sample, along with the rationale for each.

1. Mash Bill (Version A). A distiller's 'mash bill' is the grain types and proportion of each used in a particular whiskey's mash, i.e., its recipe. All of the following are bourbons, but with very different mash bills. Old Charter (OC) has a very high percentage of corn in its mash, about 86 percent, and consequently a much smaller percentage of rye than most other bourbons. Old Grand-Dad (OGD) uses a formula with more rye (about 27 percent) and proportionately less corn in it. Evan Williams (EW), at about 13 percent rye, represents the bourbon mash bill mainstream. Charter and Grand-Dad represent the two extremes. You can taste them OC-EW-OGD to experience the increasing rye influence, or in reverse order to taste the fading influence of rye and the increasing influence of corn, or do a blind tasting to see if you can identify each whiskey from its rye notes. You also may want to take it one step further by including a straight rye, such as Old Overholt.

2. Mash Bill (Version B). All bourbons, by definition, are mostly corn, usually 75 percent or more. All contain 5 to 12 percent barley malt. The rest of the mash bill is a 'flavor grain,' either rye or wheat. Here are two rye-flavored bourbons and two wheat-flavored bourbons to compare and contrast: Wild Turkey and Old Forester both use rye, Maker's Mark and Old Fitzgerald both use wheat. In addition to picking out the differences between the rye-flavored products and the wheat-flavored pair, how do the two like products differ from each other?

3. Cousins (Version A). Bourbon is the most popular American whiskey style, but not the only one. Tennessee whiskey, Kentucky whiskey and rye whiskey are its close cousins. A typical bourbon is 75 percent corn and 13 percent rye, while a typical rye is 23 percent corn and 65 percent rye. Tennessee whiskey is like bourbon in its mash and everything else, except it is filtered through deep vats of charcoal before aging. Kentucky whiskey (at least in the case of Early Times) would be bourbon but for the reuse of some barrels. Since we are primarily looking for basic style differences, I recommend using standard representatives of each type and not high proof or extra aged expressions. For example: Jim Beam white label (bourbon), Old Overholt (rye), George Dickel white label (Tennessee whiskey) and Early Times (Kentucky whiskey). To add a fifth selection, you might sneak in an American blend such as Seagram's Seven Crown.

4. Cousins (Version B). If money is no object, why not taste the exemplars of each American whiskey type? To give your budget a little break, you only have to buy three bottles as there is no super-premium Kentucky whiskey. Suggested representatives of each type are: Wild Turkey Kentucky Spirit or Blanton's (bourbon), Jack Daniel's Single Barrel (Tennessee whiskey) and Van Winkle Family Reserve or Sazerac Rye (rye). Since both Kentucky Spirit and Blanton's are rye-flavored bourbons, you might want to add a super-premium wheat-flavored bourbon such as Weller Centennial or Very Special Old Fitzgerald.

5. City v. Country. This suite could also be called 'masonry v. steel,' as most city warehouses are made of brick, while most in the country are made of wood covered with a thin skin of corrugated steel. Old Forester and Old Charter are two fine examples of city bourbons, made and aged in Louisville and Frankfort, respectively. Wild Turkey and Maker's Mark are two country bourbons, made in Lawrenceburg and Loretto respectively. If you want to confuse the issue, throw in Woodford Reserve, which is aged in the country but in stone and masonry rackhouses.

6. Age v. Youth. How much does wood affect the taste of a bourbon? To find out, taste the same whiskey at several different ages. Jim Beam makes it easy because they have so many different bottlings. Standard Jim Beam (the white label) is 4 years old, Jim Beam black label is 8 years old and Knob Creek is the same whiskey at 9 years old. Another possibility is this suite from Heaven Hill: Henry McKenna (4 years), Evan

Williams (7 years) and Elijah Craig (12 years). You can also do this with Old Charter, which has 8-, 10-, 12- and 13-year-old expressions available. For a real hoot, include Georgia Moon corn whiskey in any of these suites as an example of what green whiskey tastes like right from the still. Georgia Moon doesn't contain as much rye as most bourbons, but it is the best approximation of un-aged bourbon you can buy.

7. **Bottled-in-Bond.** Until the 1950s, bottled-in-bond bourbon (also called bonded bourbon) was virtually the only kind available. Though the term refers to bonded warehouses and the law that regulates them, it mainly means 100-proof bourbon (50 percent alcohol by volume), the way all bourbon used to be. Bonded bourbons must also be the product of a single distillery, distiller and distilling season, so they are similar in that respect to single barrel bourbons. Wild Turkey, at 101 proof and readily available, can be in this suite even though it is not technically a bond. Other candidates include Old Grand-Dad Bond (the leading true bond), Knob Creek, W.L. Weller Centennial., J.W. Dant, Eagle Rare, Very Old Barton and Old Ezra. Pick three or four of these for your tasting, depending on availability and personal preferences. If you want to limit yourself to true bonds, look for the words 'bonded' or 'bottled in bond' on the label. A variation would be to compare two bonds against two non-bonds, especially to see if you can detect differences other than proof.

8. **Best Buys.** Some inexpensive bourbons are very good and since most of us can't afford to drink Blanton's every day, a comparative tasting is a good way to determine which affordable bourbons you like

best. Who is best on the bottom shelf? Here are several candidates that should be available in most areas, each from a different distillery: Ancient Age, Ten High, Old Crow, and Henry McKenna. Feel free to substitute the cheapest local store brand you can find for one of the suggested brands, so long as it says 'bourbon' on the label. (In other words, beware of blends.)

9. **Bourbons of Tomorrow.** The most exciting thing to happen to American whiskey in recent years has been the development of the super-premium or luxury segment. Within that segment, most of the action recently has been at its lower end, among products costing between $20 and $30 a bottle. Just about every major producer now has a product in this segment. They are becoming widely available and many believe they represent the future of the bourbon category. This is a good way to taste the best efforts from each distillery. Choose any three or four of the following: Jim Beam's Knob Creek, Brown-Forman's Woodford Reserve, Buffalo Trace's Eagle Rare Single Barrel, Diageo's Bulleit, Heaven Hill's Evan Williams Single Barrel Vintage, Pernod Ricard's Wild Turkey Russell's Reserve, and Allied-Domecq's Maker's Mark.

Tasting Tips. Here are some general tips for getting the most out of any tasting experience. They apply equally if you are tasting all by yourself or with a group, either a single whiskey or a suite.

Age and Proof. Unless comparing age or proof differences is the point of your tasting, try to match age and proof as much as possible. Age and proof differences can easily overpower more subtle distinctions, like mash bill. The recommendations above took this into consideration. Unless otherwise noted, the recommended expression of a suggested brand is the standard one, which should have the added advantage of being easiest to find. Age is obviously something you have to handle in the purchasing. Whiskies with no age stated on their label are typically between four and six years old. Be careful, though, because some inexpensive whiskies may be less than four years old. If they are they must reveal their age somewhere on the label, but you may have to hunt for it. It may be expressed in months rather than years, just to make you think.

Dilution. If you happen to be tasting a group of whiskies that vary significantly in proof, don't hesitate to dilute the higher proof selections with room temperature water to bring them down to the same proof as the lower proof selections. Otherwise you primarily will be tasting the proof difference and not the other characteristics. Even if all of the products in your suite are the same bottle proof, there is nothing wrong with diluting them further using room temperature water. Even at 80 proof, alcohol can overpower other scents and flavors. Dilution preserves your taste and smell receptors and makes it easier to detect some of the subtleties. This may seem counter-intuitive, but it is true. You can dilute up to a one-to-one ratio and still detect most of the flavors present. It is common to add a little water before nosing and a little more before tasting. If you are hosting a tasting and want to provide a uniform proof for each guest's sample, mix whiskey and water together in a pitcher and pour your samples from that. The formula for dilution is as follows: (amount of whiskey) x ((bottle proof/target proof) -1) = amount of water to add. For example, to reduce 100 proof whiskey to 80 proof add 2 ounces of water to 8 ounces of whiskey [8 x ((100/80) -1) = 2]. So if the starting proof is 90 you add 1 ounce of water, if the starting proof is 94 you add 1.4 ounces, and if the starting proof is 86 you add 0.6 ounces to 8 ounces of whiskey. You can provide your guests with initial samples at a uniform proof and also provide room temperature water so they can dilute them further to their personal taste.

Blind or Not. There are many different ways to spin a comparative tasting, depending on your panel (i.e., the friends who will be tasting with you). Some people swear by blind tastings. The principle of blind tasting is that you are given little or no information in advance about what you are going to taste. Using the suites above you might, for example, know that you will be comparing wheat-recipe bourbons to rye-recipe bourbons, but you won't know which is which until the end. This adds a competitive dimension to the tasting. Typically, the host will write what each glass contains on a piece of tape affixed to the underside of the glass.

Glassware. You want to use something that will concentrate the aroma, so a glass that turns in at the top, like a snifter, is great. Wine glasses are also good and there are even specialized whiskey nosing glasses designed for this purpose. In lieu of something with a turned-in rim, any glass with a small diameter and high sides is good, such as a small tumbler. Something like a shot glass is not so good. Ideally you will be able to use one type and size of glass throughout your tasting. Since you want to evaluate the whiskey's appearance, clear glass is preferred. If you are having a lot of people you may be tempted to use paper or plastic glasses, but this urge should be resisted. Consider renting suitable glassware from a party supply house instead.

Rankings and Ratings. Some people love to rank things so if you and your panel want to choose a favorite from among the brands tasted, fine, but don't make that the entire focus of your discussion. Likewise if you want to give numerical ratings, be my guest. I don't care for that sort of thing myself (more on that later). Instead of worrying about rankings and ratings, explore the complex flavor sensations careful tasting can reveal. What characteristics did you notice in the nose, on the tongue, in the finish? Compare and contrast your observations with those of the other panelists. "Which one is the best?" is really a much less interesting question than you might imagine.

The 4-Step Tasting Process. For each whiskey you are tasting, you should evaluate its appearance, its smell ('nose' is the preferred term), its taste and its finish. You can go through all four steps with each whiskey in turn, or cover appearance for all of them, then nose, etc. Take notes. These are difficult sensations to remember and even if you aren't planning to publish your results, your notes will help you get more out of the discussion, especially if you want to make comparisons.

Appearance. Look at the whiskey against a white napkin or a white sheet of paper. Tilt the glass so you are looking at the whiskey through its thinnest edge. You are looking for hue, density, darkness or lightness, and clarity. The color of American whiskey usually runs through red into the amber/brown spectrum, sometimes to yellow or orange. Also look at the whiskey's 'legs' (the streaks down the inside of the glass after you swirl it). These indicate body.

Nose. Spend most of your time nosing the spirit. We 'taste' primarily with our sense of smell. This is especially true with something as volatile as alcohol. See what you can detect with your nose above the rim of the glass, then feel free to put your nose in below the rim, as close to the spirit as possible. Even after you begin drinking, continue to nose the spirit as well.

Taste. This step is really a continuation of nosing, even though you take some liquid into your mouth. Take a very small sip. Hold it in your mouth for a few seconds and then let it roll off the sides of the tongue. As you do that, inhale through your mouth. Do this carefully. If you aren't used to it, or try it with a high proof spirit, it can be a bit of a shock. Then take a normal sip and let it roll across and off the back of your tongue, contemplating a moment before swallowing, again leaving your mouth slightly open and inhaling. Now close your mouth and swirl your tongue around, licking the whiskey off the other surfaces. Take another sip and roll it around in your mouth before swallowing. As you try these techniques, you will discover others that will help you tease out different sensations.

Finish. This is, literally, the aftertaste. One way to get it is to swallow a second time. Some whiskies will taste sweet but then have a slightly bitter aftertaste. Some will have a clean finish, meaning little or no aftertaste. Don't neglect the finish. It can be one of the best parts.

Tasting notes. Tasting notes, whether just for your own immediate recall purposes or for writing a review, are equal parts science and art. Although some of the flavors you may detect—such as corn, wood and even vanilla—are actually present in the whiskey, most are not. You will often see references to 'citrus fruit, 'old tobacco, or 'old leather.' There is no actual fruit, and certainly no tobacco or leather, in the whiskey. Instead the taster has detected scents or flavors that remind him or her of those things. Most of the vocabulary for whiskey tasting is derived from wine tasting. The words fall into six categories: herbs and spices, flowers, fruit, candy, wood and other.

Words for Herbs and Spices. Allspice, anise, basil, caraway, cinnamon, clove, cumin, ginger, mint, nutmeg, oregano, pepper, vanilla. (Obviously, any word for any herb or spice can be used, but these are the ones American whiskey tasters most often detect.)

Words for Flowers. Floral, perfumed, violet. (Personally, I sometimes get a floral or perfume sensation, but rarely a specific flower. I included violet because it specifically appears in some whiskey tasting vocabularies. If you detect chrysanthemum, more power to you.)

Words for Fruit. Apple, apricot, banana, blackberry, blackcurrant, candied fruit, cherry, citrus, currants, dark fruit, fig, lemon, orange, orange peel, overripe fruit, peach, persimmon, plum, raisin, tangerine. (Again, any fruit will do, but these are the ones you usually get.)

Words for Candy. Burnt sugar, burnt caramel, butter scotch, candy, caramel, honey, licorice, nougat, toffee. (Same caveat as above.)

Words for Wood. Acrid, barrel, burned, char, charcoal, oak, old wood, old wet wood, smoke, soot, wet wood, wood.

Other Words. Corn, creamed corn, grain, hazelnut, leather, malt, maple syrup, must, nut, old leather, old tobacco, peanut, rye bread, tobacco, walnut, yeast.

Although it can be useful to have a vocabulary list handy to jog your memory, don't be limited to the words on this or any other list. Remember the creative writing part. If a particular bourbon makes you think 'wet dog,' write it down. Although I didn't put them on the vocabulary list, I have detected scents like lacquer and cut hay on occasion.

An American whiskey tasting can be a fun activity for a party or other gathering, but all of the principles described above can be applied by you every time you sit down to enjoy a glass of your favorite whiskey. When you preserve the experience in writing, it's almost like every whiskey you ever tasted is still there in your liquor cabinet.

Chapter Eighteen

'Old Bernheim' and Some Other Bourbon Names You'll Never See.

I. W. Harper bourbon is not generally available in the United States but it is a major brand in Japan and other non-U.S. markets. In bourbon's heyday it was a major brand here too. I. W. Harper was created by Issac Wolfe Bernheim in 1879. The fact that he used his first two initials but baled out on the surname suggests he felt 'Harper' would sell better. Whether due to fear of prejudice or personal modesty, many men who could have put their names on whiskey bottles never did, hence we have no Max Shapira bourbon, Oscar Getz bourbon, Harry Blum bourbon nor Charlie Herbst bourbon. Men whose names *do* appear on whiskey labels include Jim Beam, Jack Daniel, George Dickel, George T. Stagg, James E. Pepper, Evan Williams, Elijah Craig, E. H. Taylor (Old Taylor), James C. Crow

(Old Crow), Julius Kessler (Kessler's), W. L. Weller, Elmer T. Lee, Booker Noe (Booker's), Baker Beam (Baker's), Basil Hayden, Jimmy Russell (Russell's Reserve), J. W. Dant, J. T. S. Brown, and 'Pappy' Van Winkle. Those are all real people after whom American whiskey brands have been named.

It is natural to tell the stories of the "names on the labels." They are good stories and there are a lot of them, but many American whiskey companies have been owned and run by individuals and families named Shapira, Getz, Abelson, Bernheim, Selliger, Roth, Herbst, and Wertheimer, names that don't appear on any labels.

Admittedly, these generally were not men who made whiskey. They were on the business side of the business, people whose skills were in finance, sales and distribution. Often they ran their distilleries from places like Cincinnati, Chicago or Milwaukee. Still, their side of the business has been around for as long as it has been a business, even back to the earliest days. They were always there and even though no one named a whiskey after them, they shaped the industry as much as those whose names we know.

Early in the 20th century, Max Shapira established a successful chain of small department stores in central Kentucky, called the Louisville Stores, which he ran with his five sons: Gary, Mose, George, Ed and David. After Prohibition ended, the Shapira brothers were approached by the founders of a new distillery in Bardstown called Old Heaven Hill Spring. The Shapiras did not have any experience making or selling whiskey but they had the one thing the old time distillers who founded Heaven Hill needed most, capital. Gradually, as more capital was needed, the Shapiras bought a larger and larger interest in the distillery.

Heaven Hill mostly sold bulk whiskey in those early days or created brands for its distributors. It had a unique business model in which new made whiskey was immediately sold to distributors. The distributor, not the distillery, owned the whiskey as it aged and realized any change in its value. This proved to be profitable for the distributors but also good for Heaven Hill, since their capital was not tied up in aging stock. Another surname that has been around Heaven Hill and involved in that side of the business almost from the beginning is Homel, and Jeff Homel still runs the sales side of Heaven Hill today. The company's first brand was Bourbon Falls. It also did and still does sell a variety of products under the Heaven Hill name, mostly in Kentucky. The success of Jack Daniel's and Jim Beam inspired many companies to use a man's name for the name of a whiskey brand. When Heaven Hill decided to follow suit, the Shapiras reached back into history and came up with Evan Williams. Later they did it again with Elijah Craig. Both men were actual 18th century Kentucky distillers. Evan Williams is Heaven Hill's leading bourbon today. In recent years the company has diversified its portfolio and now sells such products as Hpnotiq (a French import combining vodka, cognac and fruit juice), Christian Brothers Brandy, Burnetts Gin and Vodka, and Dubonnet Aperitif in addition to bourbon. Heaven Hill is still privately owned by the Shapira family. Its current president, grandson of the family patriarch, is also named Max.

Oscar Getz was a similar story. During World War II he rescued the Tom Moore Distillery in Bardstown when its investors needed more capital. He and his brother-in-law, Lester Abelson, changed the company's name to Barton (no one knows why) and ran it from their offices in Chicago, where it is still based. The company's main bourbons are Very Old Barton, Ten High and Walker's Deluxe, the latter two being brands they acquired from Hiram Walker. They also still sell a Tom Moore bourbon and one called Colonel Lee. Getz never put his or Abelson's name on a product but he was a collector of bourbon memorabilia, which evolved into a museum in the distillery's Bardstown offices. After Getz died the Oscar Getz Museum of Whiskey History was established in historic Spalding Hall in the center of Bardstown, with financial support from the Getz family. Getz's grandson, Randy, is a current Barton executive.

Harry Blum's story is similar too. His father was one of the original post-Prohibition investors in the Jim Beam Distillery. The Jim Beam bourbon brand was created after the Beams discovered they no longer owned the rights to their original brand, Old Tub. The Beams ran the distillery and were its public face, but they had no ownership stake. During World War II, when the other owners tried to sell the company to Schenley—one of the big liquor industry consolida-tors—and tried to do it behind Blum's back, he bought them out instead and became sole owner. Like Getz, Blum ran his company from offices in Chicago. In 1959 his son-in-law, Everett Kovler, succeeded him as company president. They sold the company to American Brands in 1967. Blum's name never

appeared on a Beam Company product but it does
appear on a synagogue two blocks from my Chicago
home, the Maribel and Harry Blum Community Hall of
Anshe Emet Synagogue. The Maribel and Harry Blum
Foundation is still one of the largest charitable
foundations in Illinois. The Blum-Kovler Foundation,
established by their daughter and her husband, is
even larger.

Charles Herbst, the creator of Old Fitzgerald
bourbon, was a contemporary of Isaac Bernheim.
Herbst was another one who ran his distillery interests
from a northern city, Milwaukee in his case,
concerning himself more with sales and distribution
than production. Herbst in his day was a major
wholesaler with offices all over the world. In Kentucky,
his distillers were members of the distinguished Bixler
clan, as were the distillers at Tom Moore/Barton before
and during the Getz administration. The distillery
Herbst owned was in Frankfort, Kentucky, and was
called Old Judge.

In 1884, Herbst registered the name John E.
Fitzgerald as a trademark and in 1889 he launched a
bourbon whiskey by that name, which was later
changed to Old Fitzgerald. When the brand became
successful he invented a story about how John
Fitzgerald, a distiller, had built a plant on the Kentucky
River in Frankfort in 1870. He made only premium
bourbon and sold it to railroads, steamship lines and
private clubs. Herbst even had a photograph of the
Old Fitzgerald plant, which was actually a doctored
photograph of the Old Judge distillery building taken
in 1906.

According to Claude Bixler, who worked at Old Judge with his father, Jerry, and brother, Tom, the real John Fitzgerald was no distiller, although he was a good judge of whiskey. Fitzgerald was the plant's resident 'government man,' the U.S. Treasury agent who controlled access to the bonded warehouses. Like many in his profession, Mr. Fitzgerald helped himself to a taste from time to time but he chose unusually well, so well that Herbst and his employees got in the habit of calling any particularly good barrel of whiskey 'a Fitzgerald' in his honor. When Herbst needed a name for a new premium quality straight bourbon he was introducing, Fitzgerald seemed like a natural choice. Despite good evidence that this is the true origin of the brand's name, the current owners, Heaven Hill, still prefer the other story.

Ezra Brooks is another brand, like Harper, with a name that is half real. It was launched in 1960 as a Jack Daniel's clone and its creator was Ezra Ripy. Although the Ripy name was well established in Kentucky whiskey circles, Ezra and his boss, Ed Wertheimer, apparently thought 'Ezra Brooks' looked better on the label. The Ezra Brooks brand has gone through a plethora of owners over the years and is now a property of the David Sherman Company.

But back to I. W. Bernheim, who never put his name on a bourbon bottle but who does have a whole 13,000-acre forest named after him. Bernheim Forest is a beautiful game and forest preserve south of Louisville that is coincidentally adjacent to the Jim Beam Distillery at Clermont. It is open to the public and operated as a park, but still privately owned and managed by the Isaac W. Bernheim Foundation.

Probably very few of the families who picnic there know that whiskey profits paid for their bucolic retreat. (Likewise the worshippers at Anshe Emet Synagogue.)

The I. W. Harper story begins in 1848 with the birth of Isaac Wolfe Bernheim in what is now Germany. Bernheim emigrated to America in 1867 at the age of 19, during a time when the German principalities were in turmoil due to the growing strength of Prussia and its conflict with the other great German power, Austria. Bernheim landed in an America still licking its wounds from the Civil War. He initially scratched out a living as an itinerant merchant in Wilkes-Barre, Pennsylvania. When his horse died, Bernheim decided to change careers. Two of his uncles owned a general merchandise store in Paducah, Kentucky, a booming Ohio River town, so that is where Isaac went next. Unfortunately, the uncles couldn't pay Isaac very much so he left them to work for a local whiskey wholesaler and rectifier as a bookkeeper.

When he had made enough money to send for his younger brother, Bernard, Isaac arranged for Bernard to take the bookkeeping job so he could go on the road as a salesman for the whiskey company. In 1872, at the ages of 23 and 21 respectively, Isaac and Bernard founded their own whiskey outfit, called appropriately Bernheim Brothers. The brothers started small. Their silent partner was their landlord, Mr. Elbridge Palmer, a wholesale grocer. Their first asset was a single barrel of whiskey. Other partners came and went as the business grew. In 1879, the Bernheim Bros. Co. registered a trademark for a brand of whiskey they dubbed I. W. Harper. In 1885, I. W. Harper whiskey won a gold medal at the New Orleans

Exposition, the first of several such honors for the product.

Soon the Bernheim brothers outgrew Paducah and moved their business upriver to Louisville. Because railroads could reach growing Western markets and growing cities like Chicago, they were becoming more important than rivers for shipping whiskey. Louisville had both river and railroad access, and all of the big whiskey dealers were located there, on Main Street close to the wharves. They called the street 'Whiskey Row.' Some of the merchants even laid tracks from the back doors of their establishments down to the riverfront so they could easily roll their barrels of whiskey straight down to the waiting steamboats.

The Bernheim brothers thrived in their new location. Two years later, they acquired an interest in a local distillery, part of which was later destroyed by fire. This was in the early days of the federal bonded warehouse system and the government took the position that taxes were owed from the moment the spirit left the still. Therefore, according to the feds, the Bernheims and the other owners were liable for taxes on all the whiskey that had been destroyed. Paying it would have put them out of business, so they fought Washington for 18 months and finally prevailed. The brothers then decided to build a new distillery, one they could own without any partners. They chose a site at what is now Seventh Street Road and Bernheim Lane where Louisville gives way to Shively, a suburb created by distillers to put themselves beyond the reach of Louisville's taxes and other regulations. The Bernheims ran their first mash there in April of 1897. Soon they were so prosperous they needed a much larger building on Whiskey Row for their wholesaling and rectifying business, so they built one at the corner of Main and 7th.

The good times lasted for another decade but began to ebb in 1907, when a national business panic dampened sales. Before the business could fully recover, prohibitionist forces started to win major victories that would slow and eventually stop the whiskey trade. Still, the Bernheims had enjoyed a good run. Isaac retired in 1915, at the age of 67, but he would live for another 30 years. He is buried at Bernheim Forest. During Prohibition, the Bernheim Distilling Company barely managed to stay in business by bottling and selling medicinal whiskey. In 1933, all assets of Bernheim Distilling, including the Bernheim name and I. W. Harper brand but not the distillery in Shively, were sold to Leo Gerngross and Emil Schwarzhaupt, two more names you'll never see on a whiskey bottle. Gerngross and Schwarzhaupt had just acquired a pair of distilleries in Louisville proper at 17th and Breckinridge called Belmont and Astor, which they now renamed Bernheim.

The site at 17th and Breckinridge had been home to the two whiskey plants since 1852. Belmont made bourbon, Astor made rye. In 1870 they were acquired by George Moore and Max Selliger. Moore died in 1896, but Selliger continued the business without him until Prohibition closed it down. In 1933, just months before Prohibition was repealed, Gerngross and Schwarzhaupt, two veteran whiskey brokers from Chicago, bought the distilleries from the Selliger family. Later that year they merged and renamed them. The site has been called Bernheim ever since.

Four years later Gerngross and Schwarzhaupt sold all of it to Schenley, which operated the 'new' Bernheim Distillery and marketed its I. W. Harper bourbon for many years thereafter. Ralph Dupps was the plant's chief engineer until 1958, when Schenley sent him to Tennessee to build a new distillery at Cascade Hollow for George Dickel.

In 1987, Schenley was acquired by United Distillers and Vintners (UDV), a division of Guinness. In 1991, UDV demolished Bernheim and built a new distillery on the site, which began operations the following year. In 1997, Guinness and Grand Metropolitan merged to form Diageo, which in 1999 sold the Bernheim plant, some aging whiskey and several brands to Heaven Hill, while retaining only the I. W. Harper and George Dickel labels. Heaven Hill refers to the plant as its 'Bernheim production facility,' so the name lives on, at least for now. The site is right next to the corporate offices and bottling facilities of Brown-Forman, and many visitors assume the prominent distillery there is Brown-Forman's too. Heaven Hill has long been the last whiskey firm with a sales office on Louisville's Whiskey Row and now their distillery is in Louisville too, but their corporate offices, rackhouses and bottling plant remain in Bardstown.

One valuable legacy of the 17th and Breckenridge site is its DSP number. (DSP stands for 'distilled spirits producer.') DSP numbers were first issued by the federal government during the Civil War. They indicated that a distillery was duly registered for tax purposes. In the early years of this system, each state was divided into several districts and in each district the DSP numbers started at one. Kentucky had nine districts, of which Louisville was number five. DSP numbers stayed with a location even if ownership changed. The Belmont and Astor distilleries were registered as #1 and #2 in the 5th District of Kentucky. After Prohibition, so few distilleries came back that districts were no longer needed. Distilleries could retain their previous DSP number unless there was a conflict, so Bernheim became DSP #1 after repeal and still holds that designation.

The image the American whiskey industry has always liked to cultivate is of little distilleries out in the country, passed down from father to son, within families who trace their lineage back to the birthplaces of whiskey in the Scottish Highlands or on the Emerald Isle. In reality, the American whiskey business has always been just like everything else in America, the product of many industrious individuals and families from myriad different lands and cultures.

Chapter Nineteen

A Good Story.

Myths are stories and beliefs used by a society to explain or illuminate its origins and collective worldview. In myths, forces of nature and entities from the spirit world are personified, often as heroic figures. By their nature fictional, myths embody truths that are greater than literal fact. They may refer to historical events but are not intended to be read as history. They are just good stories.

Understanding the nature and purpose of myth is essential to understanding Maker's Mark. An example: though it seems to have been abandoned recently, one device used frequently in Maker's Mark advertising has been to illustrate a story about historical events with photographs of the company's president and spokesperson, Bill Samuels Jr., in costumes playing every part. The heroes of the Maker's Mark myth are Samuels, his parents (who created the brand), and his various ancestors, most of whom have had the same name: Taylor William Samuels. (Bill Jr. is actually Taylor William Samuels VI.) In various media, Samuels and his avatars enact elements of the myth as personifications of Maker's Mark bourbon and its defining attributes. Because of the nature, power and purpose of myth, it may seem churlish to quibble about what is true or not true in the official Maker's Mark biography. With myths, literal truth is incidental, irrelevant, beside the point. The myth serves a higher truth: that Maker's Mark bourbon is the best drink in the land and I am a worthier person for drinking it.

In building up the image of Maker's Mark, Bill Samuels has also burnished the image of American straight whiskey in general. He and the creative people he employs have done a great job at both. Samuels and his late father accomplished something most people in the industry would have considered impossible a few decades ago, convince people all over the world—in the liquor trade as well as consumers—that American straight whiskey is the equal of any of the world's great spirits products. He also has managed to control the image of Maker's Mark so thoroughly that it is nearly impossible to say anything about the product without it sounding like it comes directly from a company ad or press release. I will try.

The first bottle of Maker's Mark bourbon went on sale in 1959. Seemingly everything about this new product was different: the name, the shape of the bottle, the plain label, the wax top, but most of all, the price. It was expensive. Not outrageously so, but more than most other bourbons on the shelf at the time, especially since it didn't claim extra age (it didn't claim any age) or any other tangible attribute to justify its price. It was completely different, or was it? Bourbons certainly were not all priced the same. Wild

Turkey was higher than most, so was Old Grand-Dad. Old Fitzgerald and W. L. Weller had extra-aged releases that cost more than a standard bourbon, but these were all well established brands from companies that had products at every price point. When Old Fitzgerald came out with a special 8-year-old or 12-year-old bourbon in a fancy bottle at a premium price, they knew the market would be limited and distributed it accordingly. That was not their bread and butter.

Maker's Mark, on the other hand, was trying to sell an unknown bourbon at a premium price, and it faced an uphill battle with distributors and retailers as well as consumers. It was a new product from a single product company, trying to position itself as a premium bourbon. Unfortunately, the market wasn't interested in premium bourbon. Bourbon was the working man's drink. If you wanted something fancier you drank scotch or Cognac. The world was just not clamoring for what Maker's Mark offered and the product was not an immediate success.

But instead of backing off, Maker's ramped up the message, and this was the genius part. Yes, Maker's Mark is expensive, they said, but you shouldn't drink it *in spite* of it being expensive, you should drink it *because* it is expensive, since it costs a lot to make it this good. What made Maker's Mark unique was that boldness in calling attention to its high price and making that its principal selling point at a time when the rest of the industry was racing to the bottom, cutting proof and price, and saying little about quality. The first Maker's Mark ad campaign, launched in 1965 and continuing almost unchanged for the next dozen or so years, was based on that simple proposition: "It tastes expensive...and is." Maker's Mark did not have a lot of advertising in those days but it was relentless and single-minded about its message. Patience was another virtue of the Maker's Mark team. It is doubtful that any major consumer packaged goods company—then or now—would have stayed with a product and its marketing proposition for that long with so little success to show for it. Progress was very slow. The family was financially secure and believed its strategy was right so they stayed the course. Many industry insiders regarded Maker's Mark as the hobby of a couple of rich guys, not a serious product or company. Whether it was that or not, it certainly was not making the Samuels family any richer.

The breakthrough came in 1980 when The Wall Street Journal ran a front page story about this little distillery in rural Kentucky that seemed to be doing everything wrong but making it turn out right. One strategy of the company had been to work hard to get Maker's Mark bourbon into airline beverage carts. This introduced the brand to traveling business people who then encouraged their local retailers to carry it. This was how it caught the Journal's attention. Suddenly, Maker's was the right product at the right time, emerging on the cusp of the dawning Reagan era, when too much was never enough. The Journal article was a genuine boon and it immediately became part of the Marker's Mark mythology. The company began a series of small ads in the Journal, thanking people for their response to the article and offering to help them find Maker's Mark bourbon where they lived. The ads took the form of letters, signed by Bills

Sr. and Jr., an approach that would characterize their advertising for many years to come. Maker's Mark has been hot ever since, growing at a double-digit annual rate.

In February of 2004, the Maker's Mark Distillery celebrated its 50th anniversary. The date was somewhat arbitrary. It commemorated February 26, 1954, the day Bill Samuels Sr. fired up the stills at his newly refurbished old distillery in Loretto, Kentucky, and filled his first barrel. Later that same day, in a now legendary fit of bravado, Samuels burned his family's 170-year-old 'secret' bourbon recipe. He also incinerated some drapes and almost destroyed his home, or so the story goes. The company's own web site says the recipe burning occurred more than ten years earlier, but Maker's Mark never lets facts stand in the way of a good yarn. On the official anniversary, company officials in Loretto recreated the conflagration in front of cheering fans and a phalanx of television cameras. A commemorative 50th anniversary bottling was issued.

But back to our story. The recipe burning is supposed to have actually occurred in 1943, after Samuels sold his family's former distillery in Deatsville and retired from whiskey-making. Allegedly, he quit because he was disgusted by the poor quality of the Deatsville plant's product. The facts are a little different. Bill Samuels Sr. (father of the current president) owned a minority stake in the T. W. Samuels Distillery. The controlling interest was held by Robert Block of Cincinnati, a son-in-law of Isaac Wolfe Bernheim. In 1943, when Block decided to sell the plant, Samuels tried to raise enough money to buy him out but failed and the T. W. Samuels Distillery was sold, along with the family name. Samuels took his share of the proceeds and went home. The company did make some awful whiskey after the sale due to problems with a new mash cooker. By the time the distillery closed in 1952 its whiskey had a terrible reputation, which lent credence to the Maker's Mark legend.

After he retired, the tale goes, Samuels became a home baker and while experimenting with different grain combinations in bread he developed a new bourbon recipe based on locally grown corn, malted barley and—most important of all—soft, red, gentle winter wheat instead of the traditional and harsher flavor grain, rye. This claim, that Samuels hit upon his wheat-based recipe while baking bread, is the epicenter of the brand's foundation myth. It is a genuinely terrific way to illustrate what wheat brings to a bourbon recipe compared to rye, and because more people like wheat bread than rye bread, it also is an effective way to tell people they probably will like the taste of Maker's Mark bourbon even if they don't like bourbon whiskey normally. This play for drinkers who were rejecting bourbon in droves was essential when bourbon sales started to plunge in the 1970s. But the suggestion is that Samuels invented wheated bourbon, which he most certainly did not. Bourbon mash bills that included wheat had been around for years, a fact that a person as steeped in the bourbon industry as Samuels would surely have known.

It has long been an open secret within the bourbon industry that Julian P. 'Pappy' Van Winkle, owner of the Stitzel-Weller Distillery, gave his close friend Bill

Samuels Sr. the recipe for Stitzel-Weller's Old Fitzgerald bourbon, which had long used wheat instead of rye as its flavor grain. Pappy called it a 'whisper of wheat' and he bragged about it in ads which, interestingly enough, took the form of letters signed by him. He also reportedly provided his good friend with some yeast, and other advice and assistance. According to Bill Samuels Jr., Van Winkle did provide important assistance, but that was just the beginning. "Dad was a collaborator by nature," says Samuels Jr. When he was getting started in Loretto, Samuels Sr. reached out to his many close friends in the industry, including Pappy Van Winkle and Van Winkle's son-in-law, King McClure, both of Stitzel-Weller, Dan Street of Brown-Forman, Ed Shapira of Heaven Hill, Jere Beam of Jim Beam, and others. All of them at one time or another provided yeast samples. Van Winkle provided samples of new made whiskey so Samuels Sr. and his crew could know how wheated bourbon was supposed to taste right from the still. One useful piece of information Pappy provided was that wheat mashes cannot be cooked under pressure, as rye mashes often are. Samuels Jr. says his dad always intended to make a wheat recipe bourbon because he preferred that flavor, but he had his own ideas about how to do it. Mostly his collaborators kept him out of trouble. "They kept him from going down blind alleys," says Samuels Jr.

Maker's Mark is hardly the only whiskey company to traffic in legends and myths. Dozens of labels prattle on about picturesque distilleries that don't exist and colorful characters who supposedly originated the company's whiskey recipe but who are entirely fictional. This is part of the marketing world. There are, for example, no actual Keebler elves. The problem is that American whiskey has a lot of authentic history behind it and too often companies blur the line between real history and marketing fluff. The label on Heaven Hill's Evan Williams, for example, states that Williams "is historically recognized as Kentucky's First Distiller of Bourbon," a claim recognized by no actual historians. Williams was, at least, a real person who actually did make whiskey, but he isn't a credible candidate even for Kentucky's first distiller let alone Kentucky's first distiller of bourbon. The people who conducted the original historical research into Evan Williams at Heaven Hill's then advertising agency in Louisville (when I also worked there) were amateur historians affiliated with Louisville's Filson Historical Society. They carefully hedged their version of the Williams claim, asserting that he was Kentucky's first *commercial* distiller. Since then the claim has been enhanced. A few years ago, the Evan Williams label claimed he was 'one of' the first distillers of bourbon. The current label says he was *the* first. As if that isn't bad enough, Heaven Hill makes the same claim for the namesake of another of its brands, Elijah Craig, which it calls the 'father of bourbon.' Neither claim holds water historically but, like the proprietors of Maker's Mark, the folks at Heaven Hill understand the power of a myth.

In addition to a very cleverly built mythology, Maker's Mark still does a lot of hard slogging to accumulate favorable press mentions. Recent achievements include acceptance into the Guinness World Records book as "the oldest operating bourbon distillery in the world," and being "selected as the bourbon of choice to be served at 'The Retreat Room' during the Screen Actors Guild Awards." Maker's Mark regularly gets itself into Hollywood movies, Broadway plays, and star-studded cocktail parties where it is seen being sipped by Nicole Kidman, Meryl Streep, Clint Eastwood and other A-list celebrities. Its bottles have become collectors items not because of the whiskey inside but because of the unique combinations of colors used for the dipped wax tops on limited edition bottlings, and for special bottles honoring famous racehorses.

None of this should be construed as criticism. I have great admiration for what the brand has accomplished and if the Maker's Mark story isn't a case study taught in the nation's business schools, it should be. For his part, Bill Samuels Jr. has always kept his tongue firmly in his cheek when telling and enacting his tales, whether dressed up as Jesse James (a Samuels relation was the outlaw's stepfather) or as his own mother. Some of this playful spirit seems to have vanished from the brand's marketing recently, but it probably doesn't matter. The brand now seems unstoppable and maybe it has gotten just too big for inside jokes. By the way, the whiskey is good too. Very good. You can drink it neat, but take the history with a grain of salt.

Chapter Twenty

Col. E. H. Taylor, Jr., Father of the Modern Bourbon Industry.

It may surprise you to learn that the single most significant individual in the history of American whiskey was not named Beam, Samuels, Wathen, Brown or even Dant. He had no ancestors in the whiskey business and was not even a distiller by trade. The anomalies do not end there. This individual was always addressed as 'Colonel,' but never served in the military, and was called 'Junior,' even though he wasn't named after his father. He was Colonel Edmund Haynes Taylor, Jr. and he fairly can be called the father of the modern bourbon industry.

E. H. Taylor is a significant figure in American whiskey history for many reasons. He started or operated at least seven different distilleries in his career, helped transform whiskey-making from an adjunct of farming into a major industry, pioneered modern brand marketing, and fought tirelessly for federal government protection of straight bourbon whiskey as a distinctive product. He died in his 93rd year, still active, and his long career bridged the classic and modern eras of bourbon making and marketing.

Let's get rid of some of the easy stuff first. Although he is almost always referred to as 'Colonel Taylor' in contemporary and subsequent writings about him, and was generally addressed that way especially in his later years, Col. Taylor's commission was an honorary one from the Governor of Kentucky. Taylor was a Kentucky Colonel, a genuine title but one without command authority in any military unit or police force. I am proud to say that I have the exact same claim to that title, as do thousands of other people both in and outside of the Bluegrass State. Jim Beam was another Kentucky Colonel who liked to use his title and no one ever used it better than Colonel Harlan Sanders of Kentucky Fried Chicken fame. Admittedly, the commission was a little harder to get and had a little more juice to it in their day. The other odd part of Taylor's name, the 'junior,' was added informally during his childhood to distinguish him from the uncle for whom he was named, and by whom he was later adopted and employed. His father was John Easton Taylor.

Edmund Haynes Taylor was born February 12, 1830, in Columbus, Kentucky, a small town in the far western part of the state. On the day of Taylor's birth, future president Abraham Lincoln turned 21. Their common birthday would be remarked upon by later

Taylor biographers, but he didn't need that tenuous
link to connect him to the highest strata of American
government and history. His own family tree included
two U.S. presidents, James Madison and Zachary
Taylor. Orphaned at an early age, Edmund spent most
of his childhood with various relatives. For a time he
lived with his Great Uncle Zack in Louisiana, where
General Taylor was commanding the Southwest
Department of the U.S. Army and young Edmund
attended Boyer's French School. Through his great
uncle, Edmund was also related to the sole president
of the Confederate States of America, Jefferson Davis,
who married Uncle Zachary's eldest daughter. After
Louisiana, Edmund moved to Frankfort, Kentucky,
where he was adopted by the wealthy uncle after
whom he had fortuitously been named. At age 19,
Taylor took a position at the Frankfort branch of his
uncle's bank. In his career as a banker, the younger
Taylor was responsible for opening branches of the
Bank of Kentucky in Paducah, Harrodsburg and
Versailles. The Versailles branch became his base of
operations for the balance of his banking career and it
was while there that he first developed an interest in
the whiskey industry.

During the time when E. H. Taylor was becoming
established as a banker in Versailles, the two most
prominent men in the local whiskey business were
Oscar Pepper and his master distiller, Dr. James C.
Crow, who operated out of a rural distillery on the
road between Versailles and Frankfort. At that time
there were hundreds, possibly thousands, of
practicing distillers in Kentucky and surrounding
states. Whiskey-making was still largely a small scale

domestic activity, practiced by farmers who distilled their own grain and that of their neighbors, or by millers who took grain in payment for milling services and then converted it into whiskey as a sideline. It was during this period that Kentucky's unique, corn-based whiskey came to be known as 'bourbon' and developed a good reputation in markets downriver. As demand for bourbon whiskey grew, so did the desire of producers to expand their operations, but two persistent problems held them back. One was product consistency, the problem Dr. Crow eventually solved with his sour mash process. The other was financing. That was Taylor's specialty.

We don't know much about Taylor's relationship with Dr. Crow except that they were acquainted. Crow died in 1856 leaving Pepper with a supply of Crow-made whiskey. Pepper and his distiller, William Mitchell, who had worked with Crow, continued to make whiskey using Crow's methods. During his lifetime, Dr. Crow's whiskey had become extremely well known and popular throughout the country. After his death, considering that whiskey he had personally made was still in barrels and not yet available for sale, and that Pepper and Mitchell intended to continue making whiskey using Crow's methods, it seemed reasonable and certainly desirable to continue using the Old Crow name. While this decision seems unremarkable to us today, it was one of the first instances of brand name marketing, in whiskey or any other product category. Advertising historians usually cite soap as the first category to be brand-marketed, but whiskey brands began to appear at about the same time. Old Crow and Old Pepper were among the first.

In 1860, Taylor and his bank assisted in the organization and financing of Gaines, Berry and Co., Distillers. This was Taylor's first known foray into the whiskey business. We don't know exactly what this firm did, but it had something to do with making and marketing Old Crow whiskey. Soon the nation was at war with itself and Taylor served the Union cause as a purchasing agent. The Civil War divided not just the nation but also families, including Taylor's. Several Taylors fought for the South including Zachary Taylor's only son, Richard, a Confederate general.

After the war, Edmund Taylor reorganized the Gaines, Berry firm as W. A. Gaines & Co. The principals were still William Gaines, Hiram Berry and Edmund Taylor. After the death of Oscar Pepper in 1867 the Gaines firm obtained the Pepper/Crow distillery, its whiskey stocks, and rights to both the Old Pepper and Old Crow names. Although we don't know many details, Taylor must have been close personally as well as professionally to the Pepper family because he was made the legal guardian of Oscar Pepper's 14-year-old son and heir, James. Though still a financier, Taylor was now primarily in the whiskey business. And a good business it was to be in. Transportation improvements and westward expansion were increasing the demand for Kentucky whiskey at a rapid pace.

In 1869, Taylor got involved in his second distillery venture, the O. F. C. (for 'Old Fire Copper') and Carlisle distilleries in Frankfort, which were located where Buffalo Trace stands today. Some of the old buildings, bearing the initials O. F. C., are still in use on the Buffalo Trace campus. In 1870, Taylor sold his direct interest in the Gaines company but continued to be involved with the firm. At about this same time and under the auspices of the Gaines company, he built the Hermitage Distillery in Frankfort. As a financier, Taylor's normal pattern was to participate personally in the initial financing of a distillery business, then gradually sell his interest to the other principals or to additional investors. Through this process, W. A. Gaines & Co. eventually came to be controlled by the New York firm of Paris, Allen & Co. and O. F. C. was sold entirely to Taylor's partner in that venture, George T. Stagg. Taylor's relationship with Stagg turned out to be less than friendly, however. When Taylor became over-extended, Stagg took full advantage of his partner's predicament, even to the extent of claiming ownership of Taylor's name.

Taylor's big interest outside of the whiskey business was politics. In 1871, Taylor was elected to his first term as Frankfort's mayor. The town's citizens would return him to that office every two years for the next sixteen. In 1879, Taylor built the J. Swigert Taylor Distillery, named for his middle son, on a 136-acre tract adjacent to the Old Crow Distillery. Now almost 50 years old, Taylor was through with banking and fully committed to the whiskey industry and local politics. Over the next several years he divested himself of all whiskey investments except for the J. Swigert Taylor Distillery. As he concluded his final term as Frankfort's mayor he turned his attention to building one final whiskey plant, which he would call Old Taylor, on the site of the Swigert facility. Located just outside of Frankfort near Millville, the site was originally the Johnson farm and distillery. Johnson was another distiller for whom James Crow is believed to have made whiskey. The original Old Crow/Oscar Pepper site (today's Woodford Reserve) as well as the subsequent Old Crow and Old Taylor sites are all sandwiched between Glenn's Creek Road and Glenn's Creek itself, in a narrow valley flanked by steep, wooded hills. Though just a few miles from Frankfort, the site feels isolated and remote.

Although he gave up the mayor's office in 1887, Taylor was not through with politics. He was elected to the state legislature first as a representative, then as a senator. During his time in the Kentucky senate, he depleted a significant portion of his personal fortune urging fellow lawmakers not to move the state capital from Frankfort to a larger community such as Louisville or Lexington. He was ultimately successful and Frankfort remains Kentucky's capital to this day.

To cap his career as both a whiskey man and community leader, Colonel Taylor built his Old Taylor Distillery to be a showplace. As Gerald Carson observed in his *Social History of Bourbon,* the typical distillery of that era looked like a sawmill. The fact that Taylor was demolishing the Swigert plant less than ten years after its construction is some indication of the typical distillery's permanence. Old Taylor was different. It had pergolas, reflecting pools, stone bridges, gazebos, and a limestone distillery building adorned with the turrets, towers and crenellated battlements of a medieval castle. The grounds were meticulously landscaped. The spring house was designed to evoke a Roman bath. For his annual Kentucky Derby party, Taylor would hire an entire train to bring his guests directly onto the distillery grounds. Taylor owned and operated Old Taylor for about 30 years, until it was closed by Prohibition.

In addition to his direct involvement in the founding and operation of at least seven commercial distilleries, Taylor's other contribution to the industry was his work to define and protect whiskey purity. In the bad old days before Dr. Crow introduced quality standards, various methods were used to make whiskey more palatable. Spirits of different ages from different sources might be blended in complimentary ways, inferior spirits might be redistilled or 'rectified,' and flavorings and colorings might be added. Some of these additives were more or less benign, like fruit syrups and other sweeteners, but many were hazardous to the drinker's health. One common practice was to add a little acid to the mix to make sure the concoction 'burned' as it went down the drinker's throat. The marketing of these products was just as unsavory as the products themselves. Because there were no truth-in-advertising laws, sellers were free to call their products anything they wished. It was even difficult to legally prevent an unscrupulous producer from stealing a prominent brand name outright.

Crow's technological innovations had made the production of high quality unblended whiskey practical and his practices were widely adopted, but the blenders and rectifiers continued to make their kind of whiskey too. Profits were the obvious motive. It was still much cheaper, quicker and easier to doctor inferior spirits into something approximating whiskey than it was to properly distill and age a true high quality bourbon or rye. Drinkers in the final decades of the 19th century witnessed a long-running feud between the proponents of 'pure goods,' generally large distillers led by Taylor, and distributors and retailers who had other ideas about how whiskey should be made, labeled and merchandised. Taylor's opponents ranged from unscrupulous scoundrels to legitimate businessmen, none of whom wanted to be told how to conduct their affairs. The former lied about the contents of their products and added toxic substances without concern for public health and safety. The latter were producers who, like today's makers of Scotch, Irish, Japanese and Canadian whisky—and even the makers of Cognac and other highly prized spirits—legitimately used blending techniques and limited additives to create a tastier product.

It is hard to imagine today, but in those days there was little government regulation of food production. There were no truth-in-labeling or truth-in-advertising laws and trademark protection was very weak. In part this was because a modern system of mass production and distribution, and mass marketing anchored by the widespread use of brand names, was only just emerging. People still made most of what they needed themselves and when they didn't, they usually knew the maker personally or by reputation. But that was changing. The Civil War had introduced concepts of standardization and mass production, and an improved transportation system was expanding distribution. The United States was becoming a national market. Along with soaps like Ivory and Pear's, whiskies were among the first products to be marketed nationally using brand names. Because of weak legal protection, the most popular brand names were often abused or copied outright. If someone had a popular whiskey called 'Old Washboard,' someone else might market a fake and cheekily call it 'Original Old Washboard.' This made it virtually impossible for a consumer to know which 'Old Washboard' whiskey was the actual, well-regarded original.

One early solution to this dilemma was for the distiller to brand the bottle with his personal signature. While there was very little protection available for a product name or label design, the unauthorized copying of a signature was prosecutable as forgery. This partially explains why so many whiskey brands are named after their makers and still carry a facsimile signature on their labels. But forgery and brand name misappropriation were just part of the problem. Nothing prevented a manufacturer from labeling a vile concoction of raw spirits, colorings and flavorings as 'Pure Kentucky Bourbon Whiskey, Aged 12 Years,' even though every single word printed on that label was a lie. Since the problem was worst outside the whiskey producing states, turning to the federal government for relief was the only logical recourse.

Because of excise taxes, first imposed in 1791 and made permanent during the Civil War, the federal government was already deep in the whiskey business. In 1868, to discourage moonshining and promote the growth of the legitimate distilling industry, Congress slashed the excise tax rate and established the first system of bonded warehouses. Originally, taxes were due as soon as whiskey left the still. The new bonding system deferred payments for one year, so long as the whiskey was stored in a government-supervised, bonded warehouse. The tax deferral period was gradually increased to three years, but after three years the taxes had to be paid, whether the whiskey was sold or not. This system put enormous financial pressure on distillers, especially small ones, to sell their whiskey at three years regardless of its maturity. Often the only customers for such young whiskey were unscrupulous distributors who would dilute, adulterate and mislabel it before it reached the consumer. This situation became particularly acute when a severe national economic depression in 1893 left many distillers desperate to raise money however they could, to pay their taxes and other bills.

In response to these problems, in 1894 the excise tax rate was increased for the first time in 19 years, from $0.90 to $1.10 per proof gallon, but the bonding period was increased from three to eight years and a system of warehouse receipts was developed so distillers could use their aging whiskey as collateral to raise money to pay their taxes and other expenses. This solved much of the financial problem, but still did not prevent purchasers of bulk whiskey of whatever age from taking liberties with the product. Taylor and others feared the continuation of these practices would lead to public distrust of whiskey in general. They argued for even more stringent federal regulations. Taylor found a powerful ally for his position in John G. Carlisle, a fellow Kentuckian and United States Senator who had just become Treasury Secretary in the second administration of President Grover Cleveland.

Both sides in this 'Whiskey War' had politically powerful allies. Taylor's side took the position that most of the whiskey reaching consumers wasn't really whiskey at all. In one congressional hearing it was reported that each year only about two million gallons of whiskey was retailed "in its original integrity," while 105 million gallons was used for mixing purposes and often falsely labeled. Taylor's most evocative statement during the debate was this: "It is an admitted axiom that quality recedes as cheapness advances ... the ancient Bourbon flavor has departed and the stomach groans under the dominion of the new ruler." Taylor and Carlisle's first victory together was the Bottled-in-Bond Act of 1897. It specified that in order to earn the government's 'bottled-in-bond' designation, a whiskey had to be made at one place in one season, aged at least four years in government-supervised warehouses, bottled at 100 proof, and its maker had to be truthfully identified on the label. Bottled-in-Bond whiskey was to be identified by a green stamp bearing the likeness of Secretary Carlisle. Counterfeiting of the stamp and other abuses of the Act were considered serious federal crimes. Although the Act did not guarantee quality, only authenticity, bottled-in-bond quickly became a watchword for 'the good stuff.'

At about the same time as the Bottled-in-Bond Act was moving toward passage, the battle for better trademark protection was also being waged. American distillers like Taylor's former ward, James E. Pepper, and the prominent Canadian distiller Hiram Walker led in this fight, which Taylor heartily supported.

Taylor's last battle in this long war occurred with the passage and subsequent interpretation of the Pure Food and Drug Act of 1906. Although this law, which was spearheaded by President Theodore Roosevelt, was designed to regulate a wide range of foods and drugs, whiskey was a prominent and controversial part of it. Taylor and other Kentucky distillers argued that, under the new regime, only their straight bourbon or straight rye was entitled to use the name whiskey. The blenders and rectifiers whose products still made up more than 70 percent of the whiskey market argued that their product was whiskey too, purer even than the straight product because their rectification practices reduced or eliminated the presence of fusel oils.

The government's initial interpretation of the law, made by the head of the Agriculture Department, favored the distillers. He ruled that blended or rectified whiskey had to be identified as 'compound whiskey,' 'imitation whiskey,' or 'blended whiskey.' This ruling outraged the blended whiskey forces. In 1909, President William Howard Taft issued a compromise decision allowing any spirit distilled from grain to be labeled whiskey, but requiring further clarification as to its type. The terms 'straight whiskey' and 'blended whiskey' were adopted for the two basic varieties. No one was allowed to use the term 'pure whiskey' and no one was required to use the term 'imitation whiskey.' As with all good compromises, no one was happy but it was all made moot a few years later by Prohibition. After Prohibition, strict guidelines were developed for use of the terms bourbon, rye, straight whiskey and blended whiskey. Those guidelines are still in use today.

As the 20th century began, E. H. Taylor, Jr. was in his seventies and still active in both distilling and politics. When Prohibition threatened to put him out of the whiskey business he turned his attention to raising and breeding prize Hereford cattle, introducing that breed to Kentucky. One of his famous bulls won three first prizes at the 1914 Blue Grass Fair at Lexington.

Throughout his later years, Colonel Taylor often entertained lavishly at Thistleton, his Frankfort estate, and was widely admired for his elegant wardrobe and distinguished bearing. All three of Taylor's sons, Edmund, J. Swigert, and Kenner, worked with him in the whiskey business. Kenner returned to it briefly after Prohibition by acquiring a distillery on Elkhorn Creek, but he died shortly thereafter. The plant continued to be known as the K. Taylor Distilling Co. until it was acquired by National Distillers in 1940 and became the home of Old Grand-Dad. Colonel Taylor experienced the onset of National Prohibition but he never saw its repeal. He died on January 19, 1923, less than a month before his 93rd birthday. His namesake distillery was subsequently acquired by the American Medicinal Spirits Company, one of the foundations of the National Distillers Products Company, which operated the plant until 1972, though only intermittently in its later years. The facility was still so beautiful that National often used it for parties and other special events. In 1987, National was acquired by Jim Beam, which still makes Old Taylor bourbon, after a fashion. It is essentially Jim Beam whiskey with an Old Taylor label. The Colonel would not have approved. In 1994, Jim Beam sold the Old Taylor site to a pair of entrepreneurs who said they would soon reopen it as a distillery. One of them subsequently died and nothing ever happened. The site stands idle today and in severe disrepair.

It is impossible to summarize a career like Taylor's in just a few words, but it is safe to say that the

American whiskey we enjoy today would be very different but for his efforts and influence. In his day, American blended whiskey outsold straight whiskey more than two to one. Today that ratio is reversed. Thanks to him (and the full weight and authority of the United States government), the words 'Kentucky Straight Bourbon Whiskey' mean something real and special. As more of the world comes to appreciate this unique spirit, the importance of Taylor's contribution to its heritage can only grow.

Chapter Twenty-One

Vendome.

The Place Vendôme is a famous square in Paris. In its center is a 144-foot tall bronze column topped by a statue of Napoleon. It was made from melted-down Russian and Austrian cannons captured by Napoleon's army at the Battle of Austerlitz in 1805 and was modeled after Trajan's Column in Rome. Napoleon, who controlled Rome at that time, originally wanted to move Trajan's Column to the Place Vendôme but was persuaded to erect this new column instead. It is possible that Elmore Sherman, who founded Louisville's Vendome Copper and Brass Works one-hundred years later, chose the name because Napoleon's column reminded him of Vendome's column-type whiskey stills. Or maybe he just liked the name. Either way, he established a company that has dominated its field since the early 20th century like Napoleon dominated Europe in the early 19th.

Distillation is an ancient art, discovered thousands of years ago. It was originally used to concentrate the essence of flowers and herbs for making cosmetics, perfumes and medicines. Aristotle described a distillation process for making salt water potable. The Romans distilled turpentine from pine resin. After those preliminaries, the Arabs were the first to safely and successfully distill alcohol for drinking. We don't know exactly when, but it was before the 9th century. The Arabs also are responsible for spreading this knowledge to the rest of the world. In Europe, the Middle East and China during the Middle Ages, the alchemist's quest to make gold from base metals led to improvements in distillation techniques. The first European to write about it was Arnáu of Vilanova, in the 13th century. Originally regarded as a restorative elixir, distilled alcohol was called 'water of life.' That phrase in ancient Gaelic gives us the word 'whiskey.'

The alembic, or pot still, was the first mechanism used to make this powerful and seemingly magic potion. Technically, the lower, broad part of the vessel is known as the pot, while its upper, narrow part is called the alembic. Although alembics can take many forms, the classic and most recognizable shape resembles a teardrop. To distill a spirit from fruit (fermented into wine) or grain (fermented into beer), the fermented liquid is poured into the pot, onto which the alembic top is tightly fitted. Heat is applied gently to the bottom of the pot so that most of the alcohol (which is more volatile than water) vaporizes but most of the water does not. The alcohol-laden vapor is directed out the narrow top of the alembic, where it is captured and cooled to condense it back into a liquid, one with a much higher alcohol level. This liquid is then returned to the still for another pass to concentrate it further, a process that can be repeated as many times as necessary to achieve the desired alcohol concentration.

The crucial discovery the Arabs made was that the liquid produced at the beginning and end of the process, known as the 'heads and tails,' contains high levels of poisonous methanol and must be discarded. Only the middle part of the run is pure ethanol and safe to drink. Today this is monitored by instruments, but experienced distillers know when to make the cuts by sight and smell.

Distillation is a simple process and can be accomplished using devices even more primitive than the one just described. One technique practiced on the American frontier was to use a thick, woolen blanket in place of the alembic top. When the blanket became saturated with alcohol vapors, it was wrung out and the process was repeated. A surprisingly potent spirit can be made in this way.

In the 1830s, in England, Aeneas Coffey patented a radically different kind of still consisting of two columns, each containing several compartments divided horizontally by perforated copper plates. This device and its successors have been called by various names: the Coffey still, the patent still, the continuous still and the column still. In a column still, gravity pulls fermented liquid down through the column. Steam introduced at the bottom rises and separates off the alcohol. Although the distillation principle is the same as in an alembic still, the advantage of the column still is that it does not need to be emptied and refilled. It can operate continuously, pausing only for an occasional cleaning. Although its advantages are obvious, the column still did not replace the alembic entirely. Today, distillers in Scotland and Cognac continue to favor the alembic, while the column reigns supreme in North America and most of the rest of the world. Everyone acknowledges that the column still is more efficient, but alembic proponents maintain that pot distillation produces superior flavor.

Through most of distilling history, the making of stills was not a particularly specialized art. The town coppersmith could and did make stills as well as every other type of copper cooking vessel. In America's whiskey country today, however, one company dominates the field: Vendome Copper and Brass Works. Every whiskey distillery in the U.S. except one uses a Vendome still. The sole exception is Brown-Forman's Woodford Reserve, which imported its modified alembic stills from Scotland.

Vendome's headquarters are tucked away in an old and picturesque part of downtown Louisville. The company's offices are in a converted 1835 multi-family brick townhouse and are flanked by its workshops. Vendome was founded at the dawn of the 20th century by W. Elmore Sherman. He had been working as a bookkeeper for a Cincinnati coppersmith called Hoffman Ahlers. When the managers of Hoffman Ahlers decided to shut down their Louisville branch, Sherman bought it and renamed it Vendome. His sons, Elmore Jr. and Edward, joined the business and took it over when their father retired in the 1950s. Grandsons Tom and Dick followed in 1974 and still run Vendome today. A fourth generation, the children of Tom and Dick Sherman, now work at the company.

In addition to building and maintaining distillation equipment for Kentucky's whiskey-makers and other distillers, Vendome makes kettles for beer brewing, as well as a variety of other vessels and processors for dairy, confectionary, pharmaceutical and industrial uses. Vendome also is a leading maker of large scale distillation systems for the fuel alcohol industry. The American whiskey industry would be lost without Vendome. A few years ago, when Maker's Mark decided to increase its distilling capacity, the company commissioned Vendome to make an exact duplicate of its existing system. According to David Pickerell, VP Production at Maker's Mark, they determined after several years of research that this was the best way to increase capacity without altering their product. In Kentucky distilleries, the Vendome name also appears on mash cookers, blending tanks, tail boxes and virtually anything else a distillery might need that can be fabricated from copper or stainless steel.

Vendome provides design, engineering, fabrication, installation and maintenance services. If you need to disassemble and reassemble a distillery, they can do that. They build plants for every kind of beverage alcohol as well as for industrial alcohol. They have built and installed tequila stills in Mexico and rum stills in Puerto Rico. They will even make one for you or me provided we get a commercial distilling license from the federal government first. They make a sweet little 100-gallon steam jacketed batch distillation system that is perfect for a micro-distillery. Too much? How about a 25 gallon brandy still that looks like a work of modern art? Vendome also makes modular systems for industrial alcohol production that ship on a skid, fully assembled for quick set up anywhere in the world.

Although the American whiskey industry once used to be a family business passed on from one generation to the next, it now largely is not, yet the business of making bourbon country's most crucial equipment still is, and maybe that counts for something.

Chapter Twenty-Two

Presidents Day.

America's two most iconic presidents were both in the whiskey business in a significant way. George Washington owned a distillery toward the end of his life and was possibly the largest whiskey-maker of his day. Abraham Lincoln's father was a seasonal distillery hand in Kentucky when Lincoln was a boy and as a young adult, Lincoln operated several crude frontier taverns. So far as we know, both men were light drinkers themselves and only Lincoln encountered any political criticism for his early whiskey business involvement. In Washington's day, neither making nor consuming alcohol was particularly controversial.

George Washington's Mt. Vernon distillery is in the process of being excavated and restored by archaeologists, with financial support from the distilled spirits industry. Although their work is still underway, the archaeologists are developing a detailed picture of both the physical plant and its operations. Their goal is to recreate an authentic, working 18th century distillery, which is scheduled to open in 2006.

Although the research is ongoing, what they know now is this: in 1797, Washington's distillery began operations at the instigation and under the direction of his plantation manager, James Anderson. Born and raised in Scotland, Anderson had previously operated commercial distilleries on both sides of the Atlantic. He was 51 years old when he went to work for Washington in January of 1797. Anderson recommended to Washington that they enter the whiskey-making business because Mt. Vernon already grew the necessary grains, and already had a working gristmill and abundant water supply. Today we would call that type of business model 'vertical integration.' The operation that Anderson launched in February of 1797 was a pilot plant with two stills installed in an existing building.

Happy with the results of that initial enterprise, Washington authorized construction of a new 75 by 30 foot stone distillery building, which was completed in the fall of that year. It was equipped with five copper alembic stills and a boiler. Each still had a capacity of 30 gallons. At its peak, Washington's distillery produced 11,000 gallons of whiskey a year, making it one of the largest distilleries in America at the time. An operating profit of $7,500 in 1799 made it one of the most financially successful ventures at Mt. Vernon. In addition to the gristmill and still house, the distillery complex included a cellar for storage, a malt kiln, a cooperage for making barrels, and quarters for millers, distillers, servants and slaves. It also included pens for approximately 150 hogs and cattle, which were fed the spent grain. The complex did not include aging warehouses, like a modern distillery would, because whiskey in those days was sold and largely consumed in its raw state. Nor did it include a bottling house, as whiskey was generally sold in barrels or in crockery containers provided by the purchaser, not in bottles. The design of the distillery building included some features specific to the purpose for which it was built. For example, the archaeologists have discovered a rubble subfloor of cobblestone, sandstone and mortar intended to support and stabilize the wooden floor where the fermenters stood.

In a letter to a friend, Washington explained that his distillery made whiskey from, "Rye chiefly, and Indian Corn in a certain proportion." The archaeologists believe Washington's mash bill was 60 percent rye, 35 percent corn, and 5 percent malted barley. This would make it similar to today's straight rye whiskies. Although no actual recipe has been found, the proposed mash bill is based on farm records showing how much of each type of grain was transferred from the gristmill to the distillery.

Washington died on December 13, 1799 and his distillery ceased operation soon thereafter. The specific reason for the cessation is unknown. James Anderson continued on as plantation manager until Martha Washington's death in 1802.

In October of 2003, whiskey was made at Mt. Vernon for the first time since Washington's death. A replica of a late 18th century still was fabricated for the occasion by Vendome. The Master Distillers who participated in this event were: Joseph Dangler of Virginia Gentleman, Chris Morris and Lincoln Henderson of Brown-Forman, David Pickerell of Maker's Mark, Jerry Dalton of Jim Beam, Ken Pierce of

Barton, Dave Backus of George Dickel, James Graf of Platte Valley, Jimmy Russell of Wild Turkey, Gary Nelthropp and Tom Valdes of Cruzan Rum, and Willie Ramos and Brad Hiltz of Casa Bacardi. The whiskey they produced from Washington's likely recipe is being aged in special 10-gallon barrels made by Independent Stave. It will be auctioned off to support Mt. Vernon educational projects.

Less than a decade after Washington's death, Abraham Lincoln was born to a poor farm couple in central Kentucky. Thomas Lincoln was not a very successful farmer and often took other kinds of work when it was offered. One such job was as a distillery hand. Both the Lincoln farm and the distillery where Thomas worked were on Knob Creek, in what is now LaRue County. It is said that young Abraham Lincoln often walked from his farm to the distillery to take meals to his father and sometimes helped with odd jobs around the plant. These claims most likely were enhanced by the distillery's owners, the Boone family (kin to Daniel Boone), after Lincoln became a prominent national figure. Distilleries operated at or near the Knob Creek site until 1972, including one owned by J. M. Atherton, after whom the place came to be called Athertonville.

From Kentucky, the Lincolns moved west to Indiana. Part of the purchase price for their Kentucky farm was paid in whiskey. The family lived in Indiana until Abe was 21, then moved to Illinois where Lincoln lived until he became president. Abe's first job away from his family was in New Salem, Illinois, near Springfield, as a clerk at Offutt's General Store, where he likely sold whiskey among other things. In 1832,

Lincoln ran for the state legislature and lost. After that election, he and two partners applied to the state for a retail liquor license and opened a tavern in New Salem. Lincoln lived in its back room. He may also have worked briefly in a distillery during that period. Later, Lincoln and William Berry (the senior partner in the enterprise) bought two more taverns. Because of the later influence of the temperance movement, all three establishments are euphemistically referred to as 'groceries' or 'general stores' in most Lincoln biographies, but there is little doubt that brandy, whiskey, wine and rum were the principal goods sold there, and that many customers consumed their purchases on the premises. At least one former clerk reported that liquor was the *only* thing they sold. Lincoln continued in this profession, also functioning as a postmaster and doing some surveying, until he became a lawyer in 1837 and moved to Springfield, the state capital, to practice law. He was elected to Congress in 1847 and won the presidency in 1860.

Unfortunately for Lincoln the tavern keeper, and for the rest of the whiskey industry, this same period saw the birth and growth in America of a temperance movement that eventually led to National Prohibition. In those days, drinking—especially in public in taverns—was an activity almost exclusively male while the temperance movement's membership was primarily female. The abolitionist movement (the effort to abolish slavery), the temperance movement, and the eventual women's rights movement were all different aspects of the same movement, and shared many of the same leaders and partisans. Since the new Republican Party, of which Lincoln was a founding member, was based in large part on opposition to slavery, Lincoln had to at least appear sympathetic to the movement's other major issue, the temperance cause, despite his personal background. Many of his public statements on the subject are carefully hedged, although he appears to have been a sincere temperance supporter for the most part. As president, Lincoln signed a temperance declaration that had already been adopted by most of his predecessors in that office.

'Temperance,' in Lincoln's time, meant the moderate use of alcohol, not its complete prohibition. Banning alcoholic beverages only became the movement's goal in the decades after Lincoln's death. During his political career, before the Civil War overshadowed temperance as an issue, Lincoln gave many speeches at temperance society meetings. He preached against the evils of alcohol abuse, but mainly advocated education, not government regulation. He believed people would stop abusing alcohol if they appreciated the benefits of a sober lifestyle. In other words, he was more an advocate of sobriety than an opponent of alcohol.

One close associate of Lincoln's who did not agree with him about whiskey was General Ulysses S. Grant, who President Lincoln eventually placed in command of the Union army and who is generally credited with winning the war for the North. Grant was a notorious consumer of Kentucky bourbon whiskey, for which he was often criticized. Responding to that criticism at the height of the war, Lincoln supposedly asked what brand of whiskey Grant preferred, so he could send some of it to all of his other generals. Grant eventually got into trouble with whiskey but not because of his drinking habits. During his tenure as U.S. President, many of Grant's closest aides (though not Grant himself) were implicated in a scandal known as the Whiskey Ring.

The fact that two of the most important figures in American history were involved in the whiskey business should surprise no one. Distilling was a major industry from the colonial period on, whiskey drinking was a nearly universal practice—at least among adult males—and whiskey taxes funded America's government. From 1876 until the eve of Prohibition, taxes on beverage alcohol generated fully one-half of the federal government's revenue. In addition to banning alcohol, the advocates of Prohibition sought to rewrite history and often obscured the positive role of whiskey in the nation's heritage. Certainly it is good for the image of alcohol producers and sellers to be associated with figures such as Washington and Lincoln, but it is not a stretch. The history is real.

Chapter Twenty-Three

Why Ratings Are Bull.

Many drinks publications and the experts who write for them rate the products they taste on a numerical scale or the equivalent. Ratings are bull. Here is why.

1. Producers force publications to do ratings. Drinks publications are forced to do ratings because producers and their advertising agencies adore them. Why? Because they boil an evaluation down to a number, making it easy to reproduce on advertising materials. Instead of reprinting a whole review or summarizing it, they can reduce it to: "Whiskey Scoreboard Rating: 97.5 points." Producers like to tout the scores because they know lazy consumers buy from them. Rather than read reviews, they just buy the highest number. When they serve it to their friends they say, "It got a 98," so their friends know it must be good and they should like it.

2. "All the children are above average," as Garrison Keillor says. The typical publication purports to use a 100 point scale, but has any product ever gotten a 1? A whiskey they don't like gets maybe a 79, a middling spirit gets an 85, a fine effort gets a 92, and an outstanding effort gets a 99. If no one ever gets a 1 or a 12 or a 28, then they aren't using a 100 point scale. If the low is 79 and the high is 100, that's a 21 point scale. So what? The phony 100 point scale means everyone appears to do pretty well. A producer can tout its 89 because that seems pretty good, especially if you don't know what the rest of the field got. When you were in school, 89 was a good grade, a solid B. Of course, schools have grade inflation problems too.

3. "It's All Good." A lot more people see ratings in ads and on retail displays than ever read the original review in the publication. If a product gets a score the producer doesn't like, it isn't promoted. If the producer likes a score, it is slapped on everything, along with the source, which is good publicity for the writer and the magazine. When consumers buy by number, all they see is good, better and best. As far as the consumer can tell, the raters like everything, they just like some things slightly more than others.

4.   How do they know what you've already tasted? The person who buys according to ratings is driven to taste the next highest number, but maybe what they really should taste, based on what they already have tasted and liked (or not liked), is a bourbon with extra rye, or one with no rye, or one aged more than ten years, or one aged in a lightly charred barrel, or a straight rye, or who knows what? Following the ratings won't necessarily give you a breadth of experience and the essence of connoisseurship is variety, not numerical supremacy.

5. How do they know what you like? You should drink what you like, not what someone else says you should like. Is a reviewer right and you're wrong because he is in a magazine and you're not? Absolutely! There is nothing to be gained by thinking for yourself. True happiness will only come if you conform your opinions to those of acknowledged experts. It's time to get with the program.

6. There is no better. There is no best. I've tasted a lot of different American whiskies. I can describe them to you, tell you what characteristics they express, tell you if I enjoyed them a little, a lot, or not at all. Inevitably, I have favorites, products I drink more than others. If you forced me to I probably could rank them, but every day thereafter I would want to fiddle with the order, put different products in and take others out. Am I unusually fickle? I don't think so. I just don't see how you can compare two very good but very different whiskies and say one is better than the other.

7. Sez who? Ratings, especially when a magazine presents them as the consensus of a panel, have the look and feel of something objective, like measuring how much butterfat there is in a quart of ice cream. But there is nothing about whiskey tasting that can be measured like that. Reviews are the subjective opinions of individuals and so are ratings. Has the magazine had the exact same rating panel since it started to publish its ratings? If not, how can ratings produced by different panels possibly be compared to each other? Would the panel that gave Bourbon A a 93 have given Bourbon B an 89, as the previous panel did? If a whiskey's score goes up on several succeeding panels, has it gotten better? What are they measuring? What is the standard represented by 100 points? How do you weight color versus nose versus finish? Is it always the same? These are all subjective judgments.

When you give ratings, you pretend to know something you don't. When you use ratings as a consumer, you try to get the benefits of reviews without the work of reading them. Both are cheating, and not even effectively. About the only way ratings are predictive of quality is if you can determine what the publication's floor is for a decent whiskey. If you buy above that floor rating only, your chances of buying something terrible probably are reduced, but even that safety comes at a price. You risk missing an idiosyncratic gem the panel didn't like but which suits your preferences perfectly. You can learn from the occasional bad whiskey.

All that said, here are some reviews, but no ratings.

Two Antiques and One Modern Bourbon from United Distillers.

In 1909, President William Howard Taft issued a legal decision about the meaning of the word 'whiskey.' Known as the Taft Decision, it was a major milestone in the history of American whiskey and concluded a long and bitter battle within the industry. In that same year, a distillery at the corner of 26th Street and Broadway in Louisville made a batch of whiskey that was subsequently sold to the firm of W. L. Weller and Sons. Eighteen years later, in the midst of Prohibition, Weller bottled it for sale as 'medicinal whiskey' under their Mammoth Cave brand name. Despite the intense demand for whiskey during and after Prohibition, a few cases of pint bottles from this particular batch somehow survived, unopened, until the present day.

In 1935, shortly after the repeal of Prohibition, a new distillery opened in the countryside south of Louisville. It was built by a new company known as Stitzel-Weller, a merger of the A. Ph. Stitzel Company, a distiller, and its longtime customer, W. L. Weller and Sons, a whiskey wholesaler. The new company and its new distillery were the work of Julian P. 'Pappy' Van Winkle and Alex Farnsley, the company's owners. A grand opening was held on Kentucky Derby Day, the first Saturday in May. That distillery would go on to make Old Fitzgerald, W. L. Weller and other famous Stitzel-Weller bourbons. Because the Spring distilling season ends on the last day of June, the new distillery's first run was a short one. Even so, some of that first batch, bottled eight years later as Old Fitzgerald, also survived unopened to the present day.

When I became aware of these two antique bourbons, in the Fall of 1996, they were in the custody of United Distillers, successor to Stitzel-Weller, then owned by Guinness and now by Diageo. Through the kindness of Chris Morris and Mike Veach, who were employed at United at that time, I was able to sample both precious nectars at the very location where the second whiskey was made, the Stitzel-Weller plant in Shively. Being gentlemen, Chris and Mike did not make me drink alone.

To compare the two antiques against a modern bourbon, Chris and Mike chose W. L. Weller Centennial, a 10-year-old, 100 proof bourbon also made at Stitzel-Weller, albeit 50 years later. Part of the reason for choosing the Weller Centennial was that it has more in common with the antiques than do most other modern whiskies, in ways I will describe presently. To review: the Mammoth Cave, distilled in 1909, was 18-years-old; the Old Fitzgerald, distilled in 1935, was 8-years-old; and the Weller Centennial, distilled in 1986, was 10-years-old. All three were bottled at 100 proof.

Since whiskey does not change in the bottle, even after 87 years, tasting an antique whiskey is like opening a time capsule. Any differences compared to modern counterparts are a result of differences in the processes, technology and preferences of the era. A prime example of this, apparent in the whiskies we tasted, was proof of distillation and barrel entry. Prior to Prohibition and during the period immediately after repeal, the typical distiller's objective was to distill out, enter, and bottle his whiskey at as near to 100 proof as possible. Today, distillation proof is typically much higher—150 to 160, although some are lower— and entry proof is typically near the legal maximum of 125. Also, today a bottle proof of 100 is considered high as most American straight whiskey is sold at 80 proof, the legal minimum. The modern Weller Centennial we tasted was distilled out at 130 proof, diluted to 112 proof for entry, and further diluted to 100 proof for bottling. In those ways it is about as close to the antiques as a modern whiskey gets. The significance of this is that a low distillation proof means more flavor from the fermented mash is passed through to the final spirit, just as low entry proof means the whiskey will absorb more flavor from the wood. By bottling at close to barrel proof, you pass all of that flavor along to the consumer.

So why has the practice changed over the decades? You might suspect that it was done to cut costs and increase profits, which it does, but that is a side effect, a bonus. The real reason is consumer preference. During Prohibition, American drinkers became familiar with scotch and Canadian whisky, both of which are blends, aged in used cooperage, and designed to have a much milder flavor than traditional bourbon. Of necessity, the first American whiskey sold after Prohibition also had a lighter taste profile, because fully aged whiskey was in short supply. When fully aged bourbons and other straight whiskies made the old-fashioned way—like this first run of Old Fitzgerald—began to appear a few years after repeal, American consumers rejected them. They demanded the lighter taste they had become accustomed to and American producers complied.

All of which tells us how these antique bourbons *should* taste; rich, flavorful, assertive, heavy and full-bodied. Do they? Yes, but they also taste very, very good. Sampling them was not merely a novelty, both were delicious. Although the technology, especially pre-prohibition, was much cruder than it is today, the quality of both antiques was excellent. The modern Weller, it should be said, is a very high quality whiskey as well.

Trying to be proper, and resisting tasting for as long as possible, we poured out the whiskies and examined all three. The Mammoth Cave was very dark, as you would expect after 18 years in wood, but also slightly cloudy. Most likely it was either not filtered at all or filtered lightly. Today, most bourbons are chill filtered, a process that involves chilling the spirit to just above 32°, then passing it though a filtering medium such as silk. The purpose of chill filtering is to remove amino acids that can cause the whiskey to become cloudy, especially at cool temperatures. This clouding is known as flock or chill haze. Chill filtering is not supposed to affect taste but it does. The Weller Centennial was filtered, but at room temperature, not chill filtered. It was the clearest of the three samples. The Old Fitzgerald was clear, but not quite as clear as the Weller. Next to both antiques, the Weller seemed to glow.

Smell came next. The Mammoth Cave label claimed that it was "fragrant as a rose," but there was nothing floral in its scent. The first note was of anise, or licorice. Mike explained that the term wintergreen often shows up in documents describing the taste of pre-prohibition bourbon, but back then the term was actually a reference to anise, not to mint as we might suppose today. I personally love this flavor in bourbon. The nose also communicated an oily quality and a wax or paraffin scent. Vanilla was the most prominent note from the Old Fitzgerald.

Finally, we tasted. I fully expected the Mammoth Cave to be too woody—18 years in wood is a long time for bourbon and many Prohibition-era medicinal whiskies are undrinkable for this reason—but it was not. Chris explained that this is another result of low entry proof. The whiskey gets better longer. I have tasted a few modern bourbons that had too much wood in them after ten years, and some that were undrinkable after 20. The Mammoth Cave, by contrast, was powerfully flavored but did not go too far. It had enormous mouth feel and dramatic legs. A pleasant oiliness, noted in the nose, persisted in the mouth. I started with a tiny drop and the flavor exploded on my tongue. Overall, the taste of the Mammoth Cave was surprisingly dry. Although we could not be sure, since no mash bill was provided, we suspected from its taste that the Mammoth Cave used rye as its flavor grain, which tends to produce a dryer finish. Both the Old Fitzgerald and the modern Weller used wheat as the flavor grain. I also was surprised that, with all of its flavor and at 100 proof, the Mammoth Cave was neither harsh nor hot.

On to the Old Fitzgerald. On the tongue, it revealed hints of tobacco, persimmon and light caramel, as well as the vanilla apparent in its nose. Chris observed that another overall difference between the antiques and modern bourbons is that they were likely aged in barrels made from much older trees than are available today. Wood from mature trees contains more lignin, which produces stronger vanilla, mint and anise flavors. These tastes all lingered long at the back of my tongue.

Tasting the Weller Centennial, I detected some residual yeastiness not noticed in the two antiques. Like the appearance, the taste of the Weller Centennial was also very clear and penetrating. Buttery and spicy, it showed cinnamon in particular. Someone suggested cookie dough or even Derby Pie, a local specialty that combines walnuts and chocolate.

The final verdict? Given a chance, I certainly would drink the Mammoth Cave again, because there is nothing else quite like it available today. The Old Fitzgerald, while enjoyable, was not *that* much different from its contemporary counterpart, especially if you choose the 90 proof, 12 year old version. (Since this tasting, both W.L. Weller and Old Fitzgerald have changed hands. Weller is now a product of Buffalo Trace and Fitzgerald is now a Heaven Hill brand.)

The Stitzel-Weller Distillery has always been one of my favorite places in bourbon country. I love its setting and the buildings have a wonderful harmony. Mike and Chris are two of my favorite people and *everyone* there was always very nice. Sampling two rare bourbons on a Friday afternoon in early autumn is one of my favorite activities. It was quite a lovely day. Tasting history just made it that much sweeter.

Knob Creek.

I couldn't open my first bottle of Knob Creek without an assist from my needle nose pliers. As the wax seal broke, it shattered and scattered shards of black wax around the kitchen. I was delighted! Do they make it do that on purpose? A whiskey that makes you work to open it and rewards you with a violent display is the perfect bourbon for the young, aggressive trendsetters Jim Beam Brands Co. is courting with Knob Creek. Making the bottle hard to open would be the perfect stroke. In reality, this was a one-time experience. All subsequent bottles of Knob Creek I have purchased, and there have been quite a few, have opened without incident.

Fortunately, a hard-to-open-bottle is not the *really* clever thing the marketing geniuses at Beam did. Their real coup was to make Knob Creek a truly superior whiskey; fun, challenging, intriguing, and strong evidence that America *can* produce a rich variety of whiskies from its few remaining active distilleries. After all, Jim Beam is the biggest of the big, yet here they have devised a bourbon of uncommon richness and character.

Knob Creek also makes a persuasive argument for long aging (9 years) and bottling at the traditional proof (100). The high proof contributes to an intensity of flavor that slaps you with every sip; thick, syrupy, smoky flavor you can taste to the tip of your nose. It has anise, clove, and something I can't quite put my finger on that is slightly bitter; lemon peel perhaps. The body is remarkable, viscous like a liqueur. The finish is perfect, a quick burst of charcoal followed by a rapid, tingly decay. Yet for all its bitterness and smoke, Knob Creek is also bourbon at its most pecan pie sweet.

The name Knob Creek refers to an actual creek along which Abraham Lincoln lived as a young child. Since my first taste of it, Knob Creek has been on my short list of favorite bourbons. It is one of the four Jim Beam bourbons marketed together as the Small Batch Bourbon Collection. It is the least expensive, most successful and best of the four.

Henry McKenna Single Barrel.

The original Henry McKenna Distillery was located in the small town of Fairfield, Kentucky, about ten miles north of Bardstown. It was established in 1855 by

Henry McKenna, an Irish immigrant who also had a flour mill on his farm. His sons; Jim, Dan and Stafford, succeeded him. The company came back after Prohibition still in family hands. Several members of the Bixler family were also involved as distillers and other employees. Seagrams bought it in 1942, operated it for a few decades, and closed it for good, like so many others, in the early 1970s.

The brand, however, lived on, first under Seagrams which made it at their Lawrenceburg, Kentucky, plant and then under Heaven Hill, where it remains today. In 1995, Heaven Hill decided to attach the McKenna name to a new super-premium, single barrel bourbon. It is 10 years old and 100 proof. It is also labeled 'bottled-in-bond,' but since it is a single barrel bourbon, the 'bottled-in-bond' designation doesn't really add much. Before I tell you about the whiskey, a few words about the package. It is very nice, combining paper, foil, copper, velour and faux leather. The front label is actually a small folder with the product story inside. The barrel number and entry date are handwritten in gold leaf on a faux leather strip. It may sound overdone, but the effect is actually quite handsome.

Now the whiskey. It has a beautiful, deep ochre color, like the last moments of sunset. When I poured it into the snifter, the aroma ambushed me. Even at arm's length, I could smell the distillery on the day when barrels are dumped. Ten years in wood is a long time and this whiskey desperately wanted out. Some high proof spirits go down easily neat but this one does not. It needs a little water to soften the heady combination of alcohol and char. After a little dilution, you can detect herbal, nut and candy notes, the later tending more toward butterscotch than the typical caramel. The herbal qualities suggest basil or even oregano, with a hint of roasted walnuts.

Because of its age, this is a somber whiskey, deep and hearty. It demands to be taken seriously, but rewards your attention with complexity and muscular assertiveness.

Bulleit Bourbon.

Once again, bourbon drinkers will need to overlook a dubious brand personality to experience a very good whiskey.

In the case of Bulleit Bourbon, this is the second time such forbearance has been required. In 1995, Tom Bulleit released two bourbons, Bulleit and Thoroughbred, made at what is now the Buffalo Trace Distillery. That time around, the Kentucky tax attorney talked about growing up in Louisville and working at the old Bernheim Distillery on summer vacations. From that experience, making his own bourbon became a lifetime ambition. Those products were billed as 're-engineered' bourbon because a 'secret process' allowed them to gain the equivalent of 8 to 10 years of age in just 4 to 6 years. Since Buffalo Trace has a couple of masonry warehouses that can be heated in winter, the 'secret' was not too difficult to crack.

The current incarnation of Bulleit, which debuted in 1999, is made at the Four Roses Distillery and positioned as 'Frontier Whiskey.' Diageo, the world's largest drinks company, has recently gotten behind the brand in a big way and is positioning it to compete against Brown-Forman's Woodford Reserve and Jim Beam's Knob Creek, the leaders in the booming luxury bourbon segment.

The Bulleit biography now has the family immigrating from France in the 18th century. We are given an Augustus Bulleit who relocates to Louisville from New Orleans, opens a tavern and uses his knowledge of brandy-making to develop a bourbon recipe. He dies in 1860 while transporting a shipment of his whiskey to New Orleans. The Bulleit Bourbon being sold today is supposedly a revival of that 150-year-old recipe. The problem with all claims about ancient family bourbon recipes is that the whiskey made back then wasn't very good. It was raw and harsh, inconsistent, and young if aged at all.

Happily, Bulleit Bourbon is nothing like the raw frontier whiskey of 150 years ago. As a product of the Four Roses Distillery, it bears many hallmarks of that brand and of the better blends formerly made by Seagrams. Its true point of difference and distinction is a high rye content. Fully 30 percent of the mash bill is rye, the highest of any bourbon currently made. Such high rye content certainly was more common before Prohibition than it is today. This gives Bulleit a legitimate claim to being an old-fashioned bourbon, but calling it frontier bourbon is neither legitimate nor desirable.

Bulleit Bourbon is 90 proof and has no age statement. Its color is on the orange side of amber, with a hint of soot. It coats the glass richly. The nose carries some heat along with smoke and violets. The high rye content is immediately apparent in the first sip. Not for nothing is rye considered the definitive flavor grain for bourbons. As much as I like wheaters, rye-recipe bourbons are always more interesting. With Bulleit, the rye flavor is so pronounced it almost could pass as a straight rye. One hallmark of any product from Four Roses is balance, all the more remarkable in Bulleit because it is a symmetry of some very strong flavors. The rye provides an earthy sharpness on top of a smooth, silky corn base. The flavor is robust and bread-like. Smoke is apparent mostly on the back of the tongue and in the finish, which is 'long and lingering,' as promised by the press release.

Tom Bulleit himself, dressed in a business suit, also belies the brand's 'frontier' imagery. His presentation is peppered with references to organoleptic analysis, alcohol bloom, and the quality management theories of Edward Deming. There ultimately is nothing wrong with having a fun brand image, unless it gets in the way of appreciating a very good whiskey.

Old Grand-Dad
114 Barrel Proof.

Old Grand-Dad 114 was one of the first barrel-proof bourbons, created long before Booker's or Wild Turkey Rare Breed. At the time, the Old Grand-Dad brand was owned by National Distillers. During the '70s and '80s, when bourbon sales plummeted, Old Grand-Dad and Old Crow, National's other major bourbon, were among the heaviest losers. OGD 114 was introduced during that period to appeal to younger drinkers, who presumably would want it for the high proof. The claim, 'bottled straight from the barrel,' that appeared on the label was mostly a rationalization for the product's strength. Whatever may have been the strategy, it did not save the company. Jim Beam acquired National in 1987. At the time of the National acquisition, Jim Beam was essentially a one brand (Jim Beam), one product (white label) company. National, in contrast, had a huge portfolio of well known but faded bourbons and other brands, among them Old Grand-Dad. For most of its newly-acquired bourbons (including Old Crow and Old Taylor), Beam planned to use its standard bourbon formula (i.e., Jim Beam), but for Old Grand-Dad it would continue to make the Old Grand-Dad formula, using a different yeast and mash bill. This was necessary because Old Grand-Dad doesn't taste like a standard bourbon. It contains more than twice as much rye as Jim Beam or most other bourbons. Fortunately, Old Grand-Dad still supported a premium price, so it was profitable even at its diminished level of sales. Jim Beam continued to make all three Old Grand-Dad expressions, the standard 86 proof, the bonded 100 proof, and the barrel proof 114. They even added one, the small batch Basil Hayden at 80 proof.

The wisdom of this decision is best demonstrated in the bonded and 114 expressions. The 114 is a solid article. Its color tends toward the orange side of amber. Its nose, unlike a straight rye, is more floral than spicy. It does have that unmistakable rye edge, and is drier than most bourbons, though still plenty sweet. Although OGD 114 does not carry an age statement, the batch I tasted may have been in the barrel too long. Not much, but there was a very slight mustiness to it that detracted from what was overall an excellent product.

There is nothing else quite like Old Grand-Dad. This is a legitimate style of bourbon that once was very popular. It is one every true bourbon adventurer will want to try.

Evan Williams Black Label.

Standard Evan Williams, the 7-year-old, 86 proof expression, is America's number two best-selling bourbon, second only to Jim Beam. Of course, the wording of this particular claim ignores Jack Daniel's, the leading American whiskey and the original inspiration for the Evan Williams brand (man's name, square bottle, black and white label). Heaven Hill, the company that makes and sells Evan Williams, promotes the brand as 7-year-old whiskey at a price usually reserved for much younger spirits. It also, until recently, was sold at 90 proof while most competitors were at 80.

Extra age and proof don't automatically make a bourbon good, but they are a good place to start. The biggest problem with most standard brands is their youth. In most cases, older is better. Evan Williams is, without question, the best value in a 7-year-old bourbon. Even at 7 years, Evan can be a little rough, but in a way many bourbon drinkers enjoy. It is not harsh, but does have an edge. That is the rye cutting through. Smokiness is another strong characteristic. Licorice comes through in the finish. Think of Evan Williams as a traditional bourbon, meant to cut through the soot of a long shift at the steel mill and be washed down with a Pabst Blue Ribbon beer. Five different members of the Beam family have been in charge of the stills at Heaven Hill since it opened in 1935. If all those Beams says this is how bourbon should taste, who am I to argue?

Evan Williams Single Barrel Vintage.

When single malt scotch took off in the U.S., bourbon producers took notice. Their problem was that bourbon was already, as a straight whiskey, about as 'single' as it was going to get. Then the folks at the Ancient Age Distillery (now Buffalo Trace) came up with the idea of bottling bourbon one barrel at a time, rather than mixing a batch of barrels together in a big tank, the usual practice. Thus Blanton's, the first single barrel bourbon, was born. Blanton's is very good, but is it good because it is single barrel? Not really. It is good because the distillery selects some of its best whiskey to become Blanton's. Still, single barrel is interesting because it is a chance to taste a singular example of a distiller's skill, because unlike most whiskey, single barrel bourbon cannot be improved in the dump tank.

After Blanton's demonstrated that drinkers liked the single barrel idea, Wild Turkey introduced one, called Kentucky Spirit. Heaven Hill also looked and saw that it was good, but they decided to go one step further. If single barrel is good, they reasoned, why not release it in batches, based on the season of distillation, and vintage date it like fine wine? That is the idea behind Evan Williams Single Barrel Vintage. The first release, entered in '86 and released in 1994, was successful so a second, from '87, was released in 1995. It soon became apparent what 'vintage bourbon' was about. It is not, as with vintage wine, about tasting the quality and character of a particular year's grain harvest. It is instead about harvesting a particularly good batch of mature whiskey from the distiller's warehouses. Buying Evan Williams Single Barrel Vintage is much like putting yourself in the chef's hands at a fine restaurant. Each year, master distiller Parker Beam goes into the racks, checks his barrels, and picks out something he hopes you will like. In approximately one year he will go back and do it again. As the series has evolved, it also has become clear that each new selection should make some kind of statement. It should show us something new about bourbon.

I reviewed the '87 vintage in early 1996. Then, in 2001, I was given a preview of the '92 vintage and a chance to re-taste the full series up to that point. In the Fall of 2003 I reviewed the '94 vintage. All four reviews follow. Consider especially my brief 1996 review of the '87 vintage, which shows that critics, too, can evolve. Compare my 1996 conclusions about the '87 to my 2001 observations of the same whiskey.

'87 vintage (tasted in 1996). Everything about this whiskey is attractive. The brilliant color of the spirit suggests highly polished brass. Its nose is floral and spicy without being cloying. The gentle proof makes straight sipping easy, which brings out its perfect balance of sweetness and smoke. A little water or ice (but go easy) brings out more of the grain flavor, which is a pleasant surprise in a mature whiskey. Overall, the impression is one of ideal harmony, a smooth and well-mannered drink, yet unmistakably bourbon, with corn and char as its most obvious constituents. This is, probably, the best bottle of bourbon Heaven Hill has ever produced.

'92 vintage (tasted in 2001). We first tasted the '92 vintage in its straight-from-the-barrel, 145-proof state. Tasting any 145-proof spirit is a powerful experience and needs to be done with care. In this case, even the tiniest of sips released an explosion of flavor, with emphasis on char and vanilla/toffee/taffy flavors. Next we were given samples of the product as it will be released, at 86.6 proof. Even reduced, this is a surprisingly huge whiskey. In discussing this new vintage, master distiller Parker Beam revealed an interesting fact. As this series has evolved, he has found himself looking for likely barrels most often in the upper reaches of his warehouses. Barrels stored in the highest racks are subjected to the greatest extremes of temperature and, arguably, the most air circulation. In Parker's assessment, this location accounts for the intense flavor profile of the '92 vintage. It also accounts for the high proof of the barrel we sampled. High proof means all flavor characteristics are intensified and focused.

'92 to '86 (tasted in 2001). Tasting all seven vintages in the range in reverse order, it is immediately apparent that each vintage has been truly distinct and the series is evolving in a discernible direction. The '92 is in the same tradition as the '90 and '91, with signature flavors even more intensified and focused. The differences are subtle but definite. Like the '90 and '91, the '92 expresses char more than anything else, but also rich vanilla, toffee, and a dash of black pepper, all of which are more focused in the '92. In contrast, the '88 and '89 feature more toffee flavor and less char. The most distinctive feature of those two vintages is their overall balance. They present a full range of harmonious flavors with none truly dominant. Though not as interesting or expressive as the later vintages, they are more approachable. Finally, the '86 and '87, while still perfectly good bourbons, are nothing special. The '86 is particularly disappointing, with a spicy nose that promises more than its thin taste can deliver.

'94 vintage (tasted in 2003). As has been true of the last three or four installments, the '94 Vintage is intensely flavorful, especially when you realize it is only 86.6 proof. The benefit of low proof is that it permits more drinkers to enjoy this whiskey neat. In the '94, the smokiness that dominates both nose and taste is just beginning to transform itself into the old leather, dark fruit and even smoked meat tones we associate with the best very old bourbons. This bourbon is nicely pitched right on that cusp, so some of both sets of qualities are revealed. The complex taste reminds me of spice cake or mince meat pie, and at another moment of root beer-flavored hard candy, and at still another the hot pastrami at Manny's on Jefferson Street. These are all pleasant associations. A sip may start like dessert but finish dry, with a slight suggestion of mint. Despite the intense, concentrated nature of the flavors, the exceptional balance that has been a hallmark of this series since 1988 continues.

Van Winkle Family Reserve Rye.

Ameria's first 'native spirit' was rum, distilled in New England from Caribbean molasses. As settlement moved inland, away from Atlantic seaports, and as increasingly successful farming operations made surplus grain available, distillation of whiskey became more common. In those days, the grain of choice was rye. Being widely planted throughout Northern Europe, rye was familiar to the colonists. Corn whiskey was produced in Kentucky and other then-Western states beginning in the late 18th century, but rye whiskey remained popular through the early 20th century. After Prohibition, preferences changed and corn-based bourbon, lighter and sweeter than rye, became America's most popular straight whiskey. A decade ago, it looked like straight rye whiskey might disappear entirely. Only a few distilleries, all in Kentucky, even made it. Then in 1998, Julian P. Van

Winkle III 'found' a stash of old rye whiskey and began to bottle it. His Family Reserve rye is 13 years old and 95.6 proof.

According to Van Winkle, this whiskey is barely legal, just meeting the federal requirement that a straight rye must have at least 51 percent of its mash from rye. Consequently, it is about 38 percent corn, twice as much as a typical straight rye. This accounts for its unusual sweetness. The rest of what makes this whiskey special is its advanced age, three times that of a typical rye. It has the big mouth feel of bourbon, but with the bite and burn of rye. Its rich color is smokier and less orange than an old bourbon. Its big nose is almost sooty. The taste too is redolent with wood, and spices like vanilla and nutmeg. The finish is smoky but otherwise clean. This whiskey is in limited supply but a definite recommendation if you can find it. This is one I keep coming back to again and again.

Fighting Cock.

I can't resist a good sales promotion gimmick, so congratulations to Louisville ad agency Red7e for catching my attention with its mailing for Heaven Hill's Fighting Cock bourbon. Fighting Cock has been around for years, sold primarily in the South, and it is successful despite minimal marketing support. In 1998, Heaven Hill re-launched it nationwide, hence the press mailing that landed on my desk. It was a white cardboard box with the words "Warning! Fighting Cock Inside!" stamped on the outside. Inside was a straw-like material bound with chicken wire and dotted with actual chicken feathers. Beneath the straw was a 50 ml bottle of the whiskey, and a bundle of press releases and other marketing materials. It was cute, clever and true to the image of the brand.

Fighting Cock is positioned as the 'bad boy' of the bourbon business. It is a mature 6 years old and an aggressive 103 proof. If Knob Creek, Blanton's and Maker's Mark are 'yuppie' bourbons, this is the opposite. The label looks like someone set off a firecracker next to the Wild Turkey mascot. Some new products try to borrow equity by imitating successful existing brands, but any resemblance between Fighting Cock and Wild Turkey would have to be regarded as satirical.

Fighting Cock bourbon is orange in color and not as dark as you might expect for this age and proof. Behind a powerful alcohol aroma are hints of tangerine and ginger. The taste is like eating cotton candy while smoking Winstons, sweetness and char in almost equal measure. Despite its age this whiskey has bite, as it probably should. You wouldn't expect a whiskey named 'Fighting Cock' to be timid. Even if Bubba wants to cut it with Coke, the flavor of the bourbon will still come through. The finish has a very pleasant, coffee ice cream quality. Although you don't often think about 'breathing' a bourbon, Fighting Cock benefits from 15 minutes or so in the glass. Some of the alcohol evaporates and it is easier to detect the more subtle flavors and aromas.

Fighting Cock is not a big departure from other Heaven Hill bourbons, but it is another expression and worth a taste.

Wild Turkey Kentucky Spirit.

The people who steer the Wild Turkey brand have always gone their own way. They were, for example, the last major bourbon to introduce a lower proof expression. Wild Turkey 101 was the only version available for many years and it continues to be the brand's flagship. Perhaps because Wild Turkey held to a high proof longer than everyone else, it gained a reputation in some quarters as a hard drinking whiskey. An unsolicited endorsement by Kentucky native and original 'gonzo' journalist Hunter S. Thompson fueled its mystique. At Wild Turkey, they saw things a little differently. They simply were maintaining the product as a top quality, traditional Kentucky sipping whiskey, with a premium price to prove it. As further evidence they point to the fact that Wild Turkey is distilled at a low proof and aged in heavily charred barrels, the way most bourbon used to be. It also used to be an 8-year-old bourbon, aged twice as long as most standard brands. (Standard Wild Turkey no longer makes an age claim.) The bottles were even finished with an old-fashioned cork, not a screw cap.

In 1994, following several other line extensions, Kentucky Spirit was introduced as the top-of-the-line Turkey. It is a single barrel bourbon, bottled at 101 proof with no age statement. It comes in a very attractive decanter-type bottle with scalloped shoulders and a heavy, pewter-topped cork stopper. Single barrel whiskey lets a distiller showcase his finest work, and Kentucky Spirit does not disappoint. The color is a lovely orange-amber and though filtration (or lack thereof) is not mentioned in the promotional materials, visible sediment in my bottle suggests that little or no filtration is done. Remarkably complex, especially in the finish, the whiskey is well balanced and surprisingly drinkable straight, despite its proof. Vanilla is very apparent, with licorice behind it. The liquor is full-bodied but not heavy. Kentucky Spirit is without a doubt one of the best bourbons on the market, a worthy rival to Blanton's and Jim Beam's Small Batch Collection, and priced accordingly. Is it worth it? Happily, even the priciest bourbons are bargains compared to imported spirits so, yes, I would say it is.

Wild Turkey Russell's Reserve.

Like many distilleries in recent years, Wild Turkey has made a certain amount of hay promoting its Master Distiller, Jimmy Russell, including by putting his name on a bottle. Russell has been a good spokesperson for Wild Turkey, advancing its image as an old-fashioned, full-flavored bourbon distilled at low proof and using the deepest barrel char available. These practices give every Wild Turkey expression huge body and full, rich taste. Russell's Reserve is solidly within that tradition. It is ten years old and 101 proof. Its color is the rich, orange-to-brown amber we expect. We also expect it to be very drinkable despite its proof and it is. While alcohol is immediately apparent in the nose, so is rich, buttery caramel overlaid with earthy pipe tobacco. The taste reveals subtle notes of cumin, lemon and black pepper.

We expect good, even great whiskey from Wild Turkey. They haven't had a dud yet except for the 80 proof version, an unfortunate but probably necessary bow to the marketplace. So the real triumph of Russell's Reserve is not that it is so good, but that it is so good for the price. At around $20, Wild Turkey has positioned Russell's Reserve in the range of affordable super-premiums, a segment pioneered by Jim Beam's Knob Creek and now occupied by Woodford Reserve, Evan Williams Single Barrel, Buffalo Trace, Bulleit and other outstanding products in the $20 to $30 price range. We like this price range. It allows distillers (and the rest of the distribution channel) to sell a superior product and also realize a fair profit. As usual, Wild Turkey is providing a good example of how it should be done.

Old Forester.

We probably should be grateful that Old Forester is still around. If sales results were the sole criteria, it wouldn't be, but something else is at work. Look at the label, the answer is there in the signature below the handwritten text: George Garvin Brown. He founded Brown-Forman and the family dynasty that still runs the company. It is comforting to know that even a huge corporation like Brown-Forman can be sentimental. Old Forester is still around because it is the product on which the company was built.

Old Forester was born in 1870 as the first American whiskey sold exclusively in bottles. Brown bought his whiskey from distillers like John Atherton and Ben Mattingly. He prided himself on his skill at selecting and blending several straight whiskies to create his brand. In those days before modern production control methods, many believed this was the only way to produce a whiskey of consistently high quality. In 1902, Brown bought Ben Mattingly's distillery in St. Mary's, Kentucky, and became a distiller.

George Brown died in 1917 and control of the company passed to his sons. Their descendants still run Brown-Forman today. (Forman was a brief and minor partner who had little impact on the firm beyond giving it his name.) Until Prohibition, Old Forester was Brown-Forman's primary product. After Repeal, other brands the company acquired took the lead. Two of those, Early Times and Jack Daniel's, became the company's top selling whiskies. Today, in terms of revenue and profit, Jack Daniel's is the company's flagship brand.

Old Forester is a straight bourbon, made at the company's distillery in Shively, Kentucky. There are 86 and 100 proof expressions, as well as a limited edition called 'Birthday Bourbon.' The label still has George Brown's handwritten statement and signature. The mash bill is a standard 72 percent corn, 18 percent rye and 10 percent barley malt. The standard versions carry no age statement. I tasted the 86 proof for this review.

Old Forester's color is light amber, slightly dusky. The nose is a little hot, but not acrid. The body is medium and the taste has a toffee quality, with a hint of soot in its dry finish. That finish is evanescent as the whiskey seems to magically evaporate off the tongue.

Bourbon is generally considered the most brash of whiskies, but Old Forester's charms are subtle. It merits careful and thoughtful tasting. The two standard expressions (i.e., not the Birthday Bourbon) are generally inexpensive and a superior value.

W. L. Weller Special Reserve.

In 1849, William Larue Weller founded a whiskey rectifying and distribution business in Louisville. In 1912, his sons contracted with A. Ph. Stitzel Company, a distiller, to make whiskey for the Wellers to distribute. In 1915, John and George Weller sold the company, including the name, to two of the company's salesmen, Julian 'Pappy' Van Winkle and Alex Farnsley. After Prohibition, Van Winkle and Farnsley merged the Weller and Stitzel companies to form Stitzel-Weller.

Stitzel-Weller's primary brand was Old Fitzgerald. Its second-tier products were Weller and Rebel Yell. All three were 'wheaters,' made from a mash that used wheat instead of rye as the flavor grain. While the flavor of rye is hearty and spicy, it can produce a bitter, burning sensation, especially when the whiskey is young. Wheat contributes a mild character and slightly nutty taste, without rye's burn. Though second tier in terms of marketing, the Weller brand never skimped on quality. Special Reserve is 90 proof and 7 years old and all of the other Weller products also feature extra proof and age. The Van Winkle family sold Stitzel-Weller in 1972 and the distillery closed in 1992. The Weller brand is now owned by Sazerac and made at their Buffalo Trace Distillery.

Though not as rich as its mouth-filling cousin, Old Fitzgerald Bottled-in-Bond, Weller Special Reserve is pleasantly sweet, like a fine German Auslese wine. There is toffee on the tongue, tobacco in the nose, and fresh cut hay in the finish. Despite its proof and maturity, Weller Special Reserve is easy to drink neat. This is not a challenging bourbon, nor is it a superstar like Woodford Reserve or Blanton's. However, it is a solid representative of its type, a perfectly pleasant quaff, and with a price in the Maker's Mark/Jack Daniel's neighborhood, it is an excellent value.

Old Weller Antique.

In recent years, all of the action in the bourbon business has been in so-called luxury or super premium brands such as Blanton's, Booker's, Kentucky

Spirit, and Woodford Reserve, and specialty bottlings such as A. H. Hirsch, 'Pappy' Van Winkle and George T. Stagg. Most of these are in the $30 to $50 price range (except 'Pappy,' which is much more). How do these products justify their prices? Some boast extra age and proof, but many do not. Many, but not all, are single barrel. Most have fancy packaging. Still, it sometimes seems that the price is intended merely to make a statement about the purchaser's affluence. I buy a $50 bourbon (or $50,000 car) to show the world that I can.

To the rest of us, this leads to an inevitable question. Are there equally good whiskies available at moderate prices for people who want quality and character but whose egos are secure enough to pay a lower price? Happily, the answer is yes and one of the best examples is Old Weller Antique. This bourbon has all the qualities that should land it in the price stratosphere. It is 107 proof, aged 7 years, and very tasty. It even comes in a fancy, gold-veined bottle, yet it is priced at about $16, similar to what you would pay for Maker's Mark or Jack Daniel's Old No. 7.

Because it is a wheated bourbon, Weller Antique is not harsh, even at 107 proof. The high proof is most apparent in its nose, which benefits from the addition of water. The color is rich amber. Anise notes blend well with the deep, smoky flavor and its buttery finish lingers on the tongue.

Woodford Reserve Distiller's Select

A *Wall Street Journal* article in 2000 lauded "130-year-old family-controlled" Brown-Forman as a company that "has gone against the industry grain with favorable results." One small example of this is Woodford Reserve. While other bourbon companies create brands by slapping a new label on an existing whiskey, Brown-Forman rescued a historic distillery, invested millions in its restoration, returned it to production, used it as the springboard for a new super-premium bourbon, and only then slapped a new label on an existing whiskey.

The first distillery on the Woodford Reserve site was established by the Pepper family. James Graham and Leopold Labrot acquired it in 1878. Brown-Forman bought it from the Labrot family in 1940 and operated it until 1964. The property then sat unused until Brown-Forman reacquired it in 1995. In addition to making bourbon, the restored distillery has become a popular tourist destination.

Woodford Reserve Distiller's Select is bottled at 90.4 proof and carries no age statement. It comes in an elegant, flask-type bottle. Woodford Reserve has a polished brass color and a rich, warm, vanilla fudge nose. The taste adds notes of plum and white pepper. The richness and depth of this bourbon point out again the importance of the bourbon taster and profiler, in this case Brown-Forman's Lincoln Henderson, recently succeeded by Chris Morris. Brown-Forman has not hidden the fact that the original Woodford Reserve was Old Forester stock distilled at the company's Shively plant. Today's product is a combination of that whiskey and whiskey distilled at Woodford, carefully mixed together to maintain the original taste profile. We continue to hear rumors that the company will release whiskey distilled entirely at Woodford 'soon,' but nothing has appeared yet.

Jim Beam White Label.

Jim Beam, in its standard, white label expression, is so ubiquitous that a formal review initially seems superfluous, but that is exactly why it should be done. Jack Daniel's and Jim Beam so dominate the American whiskey market that they define American whiskey to most people in the United States and around the world. The Jim Beam Brands Company distills a lot of whiskey at two Kentucky plants and they market a wide range of bourbon brands, including Old Crow, Old Taylor and Old Grand-Dad, as well as their Small Batch Collection. There is also an 8-year-old, black label version of Jim Beam. But all of those combined are a thimble beside the ocean that is Jim Beam White. For fifty minutes of every hour the distillery runs, Jim Beam white label is what they are making.

Considering the volume of Jim Beam white label they produce and its modest price, it is amazing that it is a good as it is. This is definitely a young bourbon but not offensive as young whiskey so often can be. The harshness and edge that can characterize young whiskey, that burning sensation as it goes down, is not apparent in Jim Beam. Because Jim Beam White is so young, very little wood is evident in its flavor. Instead, it shows its vegetable roots and a foxy, almost funky, quality from its wild yeast strain. The yeast gives Jim Beam White a unique flavor not apparent in most other Beam products. The color is a nice, balanced amber, more red than orange. The nose is lightly perfumed. The mouth feel, combined with the strong vegetable taste, recalls Karo syrup, another product that exploits the sweetness of corn. At 80 proof, it is more than mild enough to drink neat. Although it is only a small statement on the back label, Jim Beam white label is one of the few 4-year-old bourbons to say so.

The next time you are in a bar and Jim Beam is your only choice, don't switch to beer or single malt. Order it neat and give it a try. It won't change your life but it just might earn your respect.

Jack Daniel's Black Label.

The same logic that dictated a serious review of Jim Beam requires one of Jack Daniel's as well, a whiskey that is so ubiquitous it has become a standard or baseline for whiskey drinkers everywhere. Tennessee Whiskey, a category Daniel's created, is distinguished from bourbon by the Lincoln County Process. Before new whiskey is barreled, it is filtered through ten feet of charcoal made from the wood of maple trees. The result is a mild flavor, ironic considering the brand's reputation as a favorite among motorcycle gangs and other tough guys. The charcoal mellowing process also explains the whiskey's lack of complexity. All of its flavors are on the surface, obvious and transparent. Careful tasting reveals little other than what is apparent from the first sip. The color of the spirit is yellow to yellow-orange. Its legs are thin but persistent. A single impression dominates the aroma: wet varnish or, possibly, shellac or lacquer. Though not entirely repulsive, it is an impression of some kind of solvent that characterizes Jack Daniel's for me. A little research tells me that all three finishes are made from resins but lacquers include derivatives of cellulose, i.e., plant fiber, which varnishes and shellacs do not. Plus the resins in shellac are derived (historically, at least) from dead insects, so I am leaning toward lacquer as the word to describe the distinctive Jack Daniel's aroma.

After working hard to get past that resin/cellulose quality, I finally detected a nice, solid oak undertone and a faint overtone of tart berries, such as juniper or quince, with a hint of orange peel. A slight mustiness was noticed at the first tasting, but did not reassert itself the second time around. The finish is pleasant, full and warm, medium dry, with no bite or burn. Try as I might, I could not tease out any additional scents, flavors or amusing metaphors. Beyond the surface impression, there just is not much there. Everything you can taste while carefully appraising the pure spirit in a snifter also comes through when it is cut with cola and ice, which actually may be part of its appeal to diehard fans. The proof of the standard Jack Daniel's black label was recently lowered to 80. It carries no age statement.

While the 'wet lacquer' remark may sound damning, I don't find Jack Daniel's offensive. A more grievous sin is that it is boring.

Early Times.

Like its stablemate Jack Daniel's, Early Times is one of a handful of non-bourbons in the bourbon category. It cannot be called bourbon because about 20 percent of it is aged in used barrels. It is also one of the youngest whiskies on the market at thirty-six months (3 years) and is bottled at 80 proof. Early Times is a Brown-Forman product but it was created, in 1860, by Jim Beam's uncle, Jack Beam. Brown-Forman acquired the brand during Prohibition and in the 1950s gave the name to a new distillery it had opened in Shively, where Early Times and Old Forester are still made today.

Early Times' color is a light, dusty amber. The nose is hot and slightly medicinal. The mouth feel is full with a nice amount of smoke, complemented by anise. Underneath there are hints of toffee and toasted almonds. The family resemblance to Brown-Forman's Old Forester and even Woodford Reserve is there, albeit only slightly. The main flaw in ET comes from its youth, which makes it a little too aggressive, a flaw only somewhat mitigated by its clean finish.

Old Fitzgerald Gold Label.

The Old Fitzgerald brand was created by Charles Herbst around 1889. During Prohibition it was sold to Pappy Van Winkle and became the flagship bourbon of his Stitzel-Weller Distillery. Today it is owned and made by Heaven Hill. It uses what Van Winkle called 'a whisper of wheat' for its flavor grain.

Old Fitzgerald's color is rich and bright amber to orange. There is some heat in the nose, but more like vanilla extract than rubbing alcohol, with a suggestion of salt water taffy. There is smoke in the flavor and a little bit of honey. Both the 80 proof Gold and bonded 100 proof Green Label expression of Old Fitzgerald elicit a lot of candy impressions. Neither carries an age statement. The bitterness of the alcohol and sweetness of the corn are offsetting if not exactly balanced, or perhaps balanced but not quite harmonious. The finish is clean.

Buffalo Trace.

The site where Buffalo Trace stands today is where great bison herds forded the Kentucky River two centuries ago. Parts of the current distillery were built in 1869 by E. H. Taylor, Jr., the great financier of the Kentucky whiskey industry. Albert Blanton went to work there in 1897, becoming plant manager in 1912. After Prohibition it was purchased by Schenley, but Blanton ran it for them. The company's flagship brand, Ancient Age, was introduced soon after. It became a successful, if undistinguished, bourbon brand. In 1983, Schenley sold the facility to a group of private investors headed by Ferdie Falk and operating under the name Age International. They became leaders in the movement to develop a market for bourbon in Japan. Their crowning achievement was the Blanton's brand. In 1992 the distillery and its brands were sold to Sazerac, a New Orleans company owned by the Goldring family. In the summer of 1999, the distillery was renamed Buffalo Trace. They hadn't intended to create a namesake brand, but after countless distillery visitors requested one, Buffalo Trace bourbon was launched.

Availability of Buffalo Trace bourbon has been and remains limited but has been growing steadily. It is an excellent product, from its packaging to the whiskey inside. The taste is strongly vegetal, typical of a younger whiskey, but well balanced. It is hearty and flavorful, not sharp nor grassy. The excellent (though a bit too long) label copy describes it as 'confident,' a good choice of words. Though clearly a bourbon and definitely tasty, Buffalo Trace demonstrates that there is more than one way for bourbon to taste. Like Blanton's, it is drier than most bourbons. This causes the complex flavors to fade quickly, so the only way to really capture them is by taking another sip. Oh well, if I must...

Elijah Craig Single Barrel.

Whenever I meet a bourbon industry old-timer, I ask whether there was more variety in the 'old days,' when there were so many more active distilleries. They invariably reply in the negative. And just as more distilleries does not necessarily equate to more variety, fewer distilleries does not automatically mean less. Variety, like everything else, is a function of consumer demand. If bourbon drinkers want variety and vote for it with their dollars (yen, pounds, euros, etc.), the distilleries will find a way to give it to them. Variety, however, carries risks. Not every offering will be successful. But the connoisseur is, by definition, someone who wants to explore the outer limits of a type. With any aged spirit (whiskey, brandy, even rum), age is a key differentiator and with some spirits, older is always better. This is not necessarily true for bourbon. Pushing a bourbon beyond eight or ten years is always a chancy proposition.

Enter Heaven Hill's Elijah Craig Single Barrel, at 18 years. Even in the darkest, coolest inner chambers of a rackhouse, 18 years is a long time for a bourbon to spend in wood. The risk is that an acrid sootiness will overpower everything else, creating something un-drinkable. In a sense, this *does* happen with Elijah Craig Single Barrel, but the result is not what I expected. This is a deep, complex, thought-provoking bourbon that challenged my assumptions about how bourbon can and should taste. Looking for the sweetness of corn? The spice of rye? The sourness of yeast? They aren't there. Instead you get soot, char, and manifestations of pipe tobacco, old leather, smoked meat and dark roasted coffee. Imagine an ancient bar whose wooden surfaces have been saturated with the smoke and sweat of a dozen generations. When you taste Elijah Craig Single Barrel, you need new words to express the dark, deep, rich, fully-stoked flavor that surprises you with every sip.

In addition to challenging fundamental ideas about what bourbon is, Elijah Craig Single Barrel also challenges any notions you may have about ranking bourbons on a continuum, this one better than that one and so forth. Where do you put Elijah Craig Single Barrel? Is it good? Yes. Is it better than this or that other bourbon? Impossible to say because it is in a class by itself. Equally, it is not for everyone. But if you have become bored with the bourbons you drink regularly, if you long for something different, give it a try. Few bourbons demand so much from the drinker and even fewer reward the effort so richly.

Baker's.

Baker Beam is Booker's Noe's less famous cousin and the bourbon that bears his name stands in the same relationship to its better known and more successful kin, Booker's bourbon. Yet another iteration of the standard Jim Beam bourbon formula, Baker's is bottled at 107 proof and 7-years-old. It expresses the foxiness of the Beam wild yeast strain more so than any Beam bourbon other than White Label. Therefore, more than Jim Beam Black Label, this is what Jim Beam bourbon tastes like when it grows up.

Clean and initially dry, with a finish that blooms sweetly on the palate, Baker's will not rock your world, but it is an enjoyable change-of-pace.

Elmer T. Lee Single Barrel.

Elmer T. Lee is the affable, soft spoken Master Distiller Emeritus of Buffalo Trace Distillery. He created Blanton's, the first single barrel bourbon. The company now markets several single barrel products, one of which bears Lee's name. Its packaging is simple but elegant; a squat, square bottle with handy grips on each side. The label and wax top are gold. The inside of the back label features a portrait of Lee that shows through to the front. The lack of an age statement is surprising in a single barrel. It doesn't necessarily mean the whiskey is young, but it likely is not old enough for an age statement to be a plus, say in the six year neighborhood. The color and taste support this suspicion. Nosing yields soot, citrus and nougat. Although at 90 proof it can be consumed straight, a few drops of water help open it up. On the tongue there is a whisper of mint, more nougat, and a bit of caramel. Though pleasant, Elmer T. Lee bourbon is no rival to

Blanton's, but at less than half Blanton's price it deserves your attention.

Ezra B. Single Barrel.

In 1880, S. O. Hackley set up a still at the mouth of Hammonds Creek in Anderson County, Kentucky. Nine years later, he took as his partner Issac 'Ike' Hoffman, who soon bought him out and named the distillery Hoffman. His leading brands were Old Hoffman and Old Spring, which were distributed by L. & E. Wertheimer, a Cincinnati whiskey broker. Hoffman went under in about 1912. Wertheimer bought the place in 1916 and kept the Hoffman name. After Prohibition the plant was rebuilt, reopened and run for Wertheimer by Robert and Ezra Ripy, two of the sons of Thomas Ripy, the dean of Anderson County distillers. In 1960 they introduced a new bourbon, Ezra Brooks, a Jack Daniel's knock-off, which sold well enough that in 1968 Wertheimer renamed the place Ezra Brooks Distilling Co. In the 1970s the distillery closed and the Ezra Brooks brand was acquired by Medley Distilling of Owensboro, Kentucky. Glenmore acquired Medley and with it Ezra Brooks in the 1980s. In the early 1990s, Ezra Brooks was sold to the David Sherman Company of St. Louis, Missouri. Since the acquisition, Sherman's major contribution has been the introduction of Ezra B, a 15-year-old, single barrel expression. Sherman is a marketer and rectifier, not a distiller, so the original source of this bourbon is unknown.

The Ezra B bottle, which seems slightly garish in the store, looks quite nice at home. It is a simple, squat, round bottle with broad shoulders. The slightly tapered neck is circled by a blue, burgundy and gold ribbon, secured to the blue, cream and gold front label by a plastic seal touting the whiskey's proof, which is 99. The bottle is cork-finished and sealed with blue wax. The barrel number and bottling date are hand-written on the front label. Inside this handsome package is a truly outstanding whiskey.

After bourbon passes about ten years in wood, the qualities it derives from the barrel's charred inner surface become dominant. Long-aged bourbons always risk being overpowered by an astringent and unpleasant sootiness. Ezra B avoids this fate with surpassing elegance. The rich complexity of long aging is there without any edge. Although intimations of dark roasted coffee, old leather, pipe tobacco and smoked meat are all present, so are offsetting floral notes and suggestions of figs, other dried fruit, and roasted chestnuts. It is relatively dry, with none of the candy notes so often found in old bourbons. Its many flavors are ideally harmonized, and the finish is long and warm.

Even at 99 proof, Ezra B is possible to sip without ice or water, but a little water doesn't hurt. While its flavor may be too intense for some drinkers, those looking for new bourbon experiences will find it a joy to study and savor. I find it the best of the over-10-years set, the perfect combination of challenge and charm. (Note: recently a 12-year-old Ezra B has begun to appear on retail shelves. It seems to be a replacement, not an addition, to the 15-year-old. I haven't tried it yet, because I am buying up as much of the 15-year-old as my budget permits. You might want to think about doing the same.)

Old Whiskey River.

Although Willie Nelson's name is on the label, Old Whiskey River bourbon is the creation of Shep Gordon, an entertainment industry impresario. Gordon's company, Alive Enterprises, has managed such diverse talents as Alice Cooper, Raquel Welch, Anne Murray, Rick James and Ben Vereen. Alive Spirits, his liquor marketing company, was involved in the launch of Sammy Hagar's Cabo Wabo Tequila. Private label bourbons usually take pains to hide the source of their whiskey, but Willie's PR for Old Whiskey River proudly announces the source as Heaven Hill. The fact that Heaven Hill is an American family-owned business ties in with Willie's famous support of family farms.

Willie's whiskey is six years old and 86 proof. The package design is clean and tasteful, with a neck strip that looks like Willie's famous bandana. An autographed guitar pick is attached. The whiskey is probably better than it needs to be for a product based on a celebrity name. Both the scent and taste are candy sweet, the smell more like nougat, the taste more like caramel. Fruit acids, like tart apple, come through in the finish. At six years, it is still young enough for you to taste grain, but old enough that there is depth from the wood. The name comes from Willie's 1978 hit song, "Whiskey River," which includes the line, "Whiskey River Don't Run Dry." Yup, that's the marketing theme. I like this product. My only complaint is the price, at almost $30 a little too high for what it is.

Old Charter 'Classic 90.'

Old Charter is a venerable brand. Its name refers to the Charter Oak, a tree in Hartford where the Connecticut colonial charter was hidden from English troops in 1687. Old Charter was launched in 1874 by Adam and Ben Chapeze, who owned a distillery in Bullitt County, Kentucky. It has passed through many owners since then. In 1999 it was sold to Sazerac, the parent company of Buffalo Trace. One of the brand's higher end expressions, the 'Classic 90' comes in an elegantly old-fashioned bottle with a stylized rendering of a rye plant pressed into the glass. Although pretty, this is an odd choice because Old Charter contains less rye than any other rye-recipe bourbon made.

At 12 years old and 90 proof, the Classic 90 deserves to be considered a super premium brand, but it isn't priced like one. It is a first rate and very enjoyable whiskey, and an excellent value. Delicate floral notes can be teased from its subtle nose. It also brings to mind a prize-winning, aged tobacco leaf at the Kentucky State Fair. Its sweetness is very pure and straightforward, with little nuance. A bit of soot remains on the finish. If you want an under-$15 bourbon you can enjoy neat, and you can find the not-widely-distributed Old Charter Classic 90, you should buy it immediately.

Corner Creek Reserve.

Ted Kraut, one of the owners of Corner Creek Distilling Co., of Miami, Florida, says he wanted to create "a bourbon that was a little different." He launched the Corner Creek brand in 1998 because he, "noticed the Bourbon category had stopped its slide and started to increase." He chose the name Corner Creek, "to create a relaxed, sipping atmosphere." He sells the product in the US, Canada, Europe and Japan. Ted's idea was to create a premium quality specialty bourbon that could be sold at a reasonable price, in this case about $20.

The Corner Creek label says it contains both wheat and rye, which makes it the only bourbon to use both flavor grains. Ted confirmed those ingredients to me and mentioned a past association with the Old Fitzgerald and W. L. Weller brands as his reason for wanting a wheated bourbon, but he wasn't able to tell me more about how the product is made. Is it a four-grain mash, or a combination of rye-recipe bourbon and wheated bourbon? Ted couldn't say, but the latter is more likely. It is unfortunate that Ted won't provide more details because four-grain bourbon is something of a holy grail among hard core bourbon fanciers.

Another way in which Corner Creek is 'a little different' is its use of a tinted, light green wine bottle. Bourbon is normally sold in clear bottles so shoppers can evaluate the color. Does Corner Creek have something to hide? Not really. Its color is a lovely amber. The whiskey is very slightly cloudy, and the label does say it is 'only lightly filtered,' so perhaps the tinted bottle was chosen to hide chill haze, something that doesn't concern most drinkers but does irritate retailers, who consider it a defect. Chill filtering, an almost universal practice with whiskey, prevents chill haze but deprives the spirit of some flavor. Although contrary to tradition, a tinted bottle solves the cosmetic problem without affecting taste, a noble solution.

Corner Creek Reserve bourbon is eight years old and 88 proof. Char and licorice, both very masculine notes, are the dominant flavors, tempered by dark chocolate. No grain character remains, although the sharp citrus finish suggests the presence of rye in the mash. It is also relatively dry. The dryness and relatively low proof balance the strong, masculine flavors to produce a whiskey that is flavorful without being heavy. It is also surprisingly refreshing, an attribute not normally applied to bourbon. The finish especially is something to savor. For several moments after you swallow, it moves from your lips to your tongue to the roof of your mouth and into the back of your throat, leaving quick impressions like snatches of blank verse. A tingle of alcohol here, a lingering whiff of smoke there. You will want to hold off on a subsequent sip to get the most of this effect.

Dry bourbons with little or no grain character are always a good choice for scotch drinkers who want to try bourbon. Blanton's, Basil Hayden and now Corner Creek are bourbons that are friendly to scotch fans.

Very Very Old Fitzgerald.

It may be cruel of me to review a bourbon that has not been readily available for more than a decade, especially since I am about to say that it very well may be the best bourbon every made. Such a claim I do not make lightly. If you cannot bear to read about such an unattainable whiskey, please skip to the next review.

Extra aged versions of Old Fitzgerald have come in many forms, ranging from 10 to 15 years, starting in the late 1950s. The brand's current owner, Heaven Hill, still makes a 12-year-old version called Very Special Old Fitzgerald. But the legendary whiskey is a 12-year-old, bottled-in-bond bourbon produced at the Stitzel-Weller Distillery during its final years under the Van Winkle family, a reign that ended in 1972. Old Fitzgerald was the flagship of the Stitzel-Weller fleet and Very Very Old Fitzgerald, with its elegant gold-veined bottle, was the pinnacle of the Old Fitz line. Even when commonly available it was promoted as a collector's item.

As a wheated bourbon, Old Fitzgerald starts with fewer rough edges than does a rye recipe brew. After twelve years in oak, it is thoroughly tamed. The nose of Very Very Old Fitzgerald is redolent of pipe tobacco. The taste combines milk chocolate and caramel in a way that might remind one of Milk Duds candy were it not for the distinct licorice undertone, and the lack of seriousness such a characterization might imply. Well-aged rye recipe bourbons tend to be dry with a herbal or citrus finish. With well-aged wheat bourbons, candy comparisons are unavoidable, but candy for grown-ups. The epitome of this, Very Very Old Fitzgerald is almost like syrup. Lip licking is not optional. It is sweet but not (unless you have no tolerance for such things) cloying. There are sophisticated sensations here in, around and underneath the profound sweetness. Because it seems to coat the mouth and has such a long finish, this is the kind of spirit some people would describe as 'chewy.'

Taste memory is notoriously volatile, but if you have ever had Very Very Old Fitzgerald you will remember exactly how it tasted. Good thing, that, since it is now almost impossible to obtain. Bottles do surface from time to time on eBay and other places. Is Very Very Old Fitzgerald, in fact, the best bourbon ever made? Taste is too subjective to make an absolute declaration, but if such a determination were possible, it would be a strong contender for the honor.

Very Old Barton.

It is easy to forget that the Barton Distillery even exists. You can see part of it from the road as you come into Bardstown from the south, on route 31 from Bluesgrass Parkway, but you can't see it from Stephen Foster Avenue (route 62), the main drag through town, even though it is just a few hundred yards due south of the St. Joseph Proto-Cathedral (built in 1819, the oldest Roman Catholic cathedral west of the Alleghenies). Glimpses of some of its rackhouses, located atop one of the town's highest hills, appear through the trees as you drive around town, but rackhouses are a familiar site in the Bardstown vicinity and you may not realize whose they are.

Barton is quiet around town too. It doesn't give public tours, it doesn't have a visitor's center. The other local and nearby distilleries, Heaven Hill, Maker's Mark and Jim Beam, are much more visible. When Barton is mashing you can smell the yeasty aroma all over town (locals call it "the smell of prosperity") but otherwise the company is pretty low key.

The site, in a small valley with easy access to water, is ideal for a distillery and there have been several at that location since the earliest dates. Two were the Mattingly and Moore Distillery and the adjacent Tom Moore Distillery. After prohibition, Tom Moore's son attempted to rebuild and reopen his father's plant. He gave up after a few years and in 1944, the remaining investors sold out to Oscar Getz, who renamed the facility Barton. Barton's best known products are

Corona Beer and Black Velvet Canadian Whiskey, but they do make, age and bottle bourbon whiskey at their distillery in Bardstown. Barton's parent company is Constellation Brands, headquartered in Fairport, New York. Their national bourbons are Ten High and Walker's Deluxe, decent but unremarkable products. Their much better bourbon is the popular regional brand, Very Old Barton. Although Barton, the company, keeps a low profile, Very Old Barton bourbon is prominent in Kentucky liquor stores, with shelf space comparable to Jim Beam White Label, Jack Daniel's Black Label, and other top national brands. In fact, it is Kentucky's best-selling bourbon. Big stores carry the full range of sizes at four different proofs, 80, 86, 90 and 100.

All of the Very Old Barton Bourbon expressions are six years old. I prefer the 100 proof bottled-in-bond. It has a nice combination of grain character and age. The grain manifests itself as a custard or creamed corn flavor. Char, while clearly present, is not overpowering and does not distract from other flavors, all of which are concentrated and intense in the 100 proof expression. Fragrant floral qualities reveal it as a rye recipe bourbon, but it is not dry. The sweet edge has echoes of pancake syrup.

Very Old Barton is popular among Kentuckians, i.e., people who really know bourbon. Too bad you have to go to Kentucky or one of the other mostly Southern states where it is sold to get a bottle. If you happen to be in the neighborhood, consider picking up a case.

Four Roses.

Until recently, Four Roses bourbon has not been available in the United States. Today it is still mostly available only in Kentucky and nearby states, but it is a major brand in Europe and Asia. Its new owner, Japan's Kirin Brewery Co. Ltd., has promised wider distribution. The only Four Roses expression currently available here is an 80 proof with no age statement. In other markets there are additional expressions, including a single barrel.

Four Roses bourbon has an unusual production method, described fully in an earlier chapter. Although it is definitely bourbon, Four Roses bears a resemblance to Crown Royal Canadian Whisky. More than any particular flavor, you are struck by its balance. Everything is in its proper place, with no characteristic overpowering any other. The color is light amber-to-orange, highly polished. The nose is warm and slightly spicy, with a hint of barbecue sauce. Peppermint and licorice appear on the tongue. The characteristic that most marks it as bourbon (as distinguished from Crown Royal) is char, which comes across as mildly astringent. This quality, combined with the peppermint, reminds me of Altoids mints.

Because Four Roses is distinctly unlike any other bourbon, the true enthusiast will want to try it. Too bad it is still so hard to get.

George T. Stagg.

When Buffalo Trace released George T. Stagg, a 15-year-old rye recipe bourbon, in October of 2002, it joined an existing group of products known as the Antique Whiskey Collection. While all of the other whiskies in that collection (Eagle Rare 17 year old rye recipe bourbon, Sazerac 18 year old rye whiskey and W.L. Weller 19 year old wheated bourbon) have been critically acclaimed and commercially successful, George T. Stagg set a new standard and has become perhaps the first true enthusiast bottling of American whiskey. By 'enthusiast bottling,' I mean a product created primarily for the small but passionate community of hard core bourbon aficionados, a product that pushes the envelope of what we understand bourbon to be, a product that by its very nature has an esoteric appeal (i.e., it's not for everyone), and a product that creates its own momentum within the enthusiast community. An enthusiast product should respect the consumer's intelligence and knowledge by being scrupulously honest on paper, respect the enthusiast's palate by performing spectacularly in the glass, and flatter the enthusiast's aesthetic sensibilities with sophisticated packaging. George T. Stagg is all of these things and, as such, raises the bar for every new American whiskey to come.

Even more remarkable than the product itself has been its sales trajectory. The 2002 release sold out almost instantly. Within a few months the distillery had exhausted its supply and the product was quickly disappearing at retail. The fact that Malt Advocate

Magazine immediately named it American Whiskey of the Year for 2002 certainly added to its luster. Knowing it would soon be gone, some enthusiasts bought it by the case, despite a retail price in the $35 to $45 per bottle range. Tips about stores that still had it in stock spread like wildfire over the internet, quickly exhausting what little retail inventory was left. The 2003 release sold out even faster.

George T. Stagg co-founded the distillery now known as Buffalo Trace in about 1869. Stagg bourbon is the first unfiltered and uncut whiskey from Buffalo Trace, and one of a very few from any company. The 2002 release came out of the barrel at a (literally) staggering 137.6 proof. The 2003 topped that at 142.7. Because of its concentration and advanced age, the color is very deep and as red as bourbon gets. Each time I have tasted Stagg, I have been struck by the scent of fresh corn that leaps off my skin as a few drops of the whiskey touch it, even before I pour any into a glass. Subsequently, that particular scent (which you don't expect in a long-aged bourbon) is elusive, replaced by a complex aroma dominated by wood. But this is not the ordinary charred oak aroma you expect from bourbon. This smells exactly like the air that greets you when you step deep inside a whiskey warehouse.

With the addition of room temperature water, the nose opens up considerably and gives you old leather, pipe tobacco and the wool of an ancient, favored sweater. Like the nose, the taste is all about intensity and complexity. It is dry with herbal notes like oregano, basil and rosemary, and black pepper spice. These are all sharp flavors and considering the high proof, it should be apparent that this is not a drink for beginners. You need a basic understanding of bourbon geography before you can fully appreciate something this far out on the edge.

George Dickel No. 12.

The George A. Dickel Cascade Hollow Distillery in Tullahoma, Tennessee, was dark for several years after parent company Diageo ditched most of its American whiskey business in 1999. It is back now. There are two products, the 80 proof No. 8 Brand (black label) and the more expensive 90 proof No. 12 Brand (white label). The No. 12 is the current marketing focus.

The color of Dickel No. 12 is a sooty orange. There is plenty of smoke in the nose, more so than on the tongue. This is a good starter whiskey because it is sweet, with no off tastes. It lacks depth and complexity, but that isn't necessarily bad. If the phrase 'pleasant and inoffensive' seems like damning with faint praise, so be it. It's still a pretty good drink, or as the Dickel folks say, "finest quality sippin' whiskey."

Eagle Rare Single Barrel.

Eagle Rare is a former Seagram's brand, acquired by the Sazerac Company in 1989. It was a post-WWII creation, designed to compete with Wild Turkey (bird theme, 101 proof). Sazerac's bourbon arm, Buffalo Trace, markets it today. The standard Eagle Rare is still 101 proof and ten years old. There is also a 17-year-old, 90 proof version in the Antique Whiskey Collection. The Single Barrel likewise is 90 proof and ten years old. Though not considered part of the Antique Whiskey Collection, it comes in a similar bottle bearing a large, screen printed silver eagle.

The color of Eagle Rare Single Barrel is light amber, nearly yellow, with just a hint of soot. The nose is candy-sweet, with caramel and licorice. The body is very big, with legs that coat the glass like syrup, suggesting what is in fact a huge mouth feel. The age is revealed in an ever-so-slight mustiness, not enough to be unpleasant but suggestive of a whiskey at its peak that would not improve with additional time in wood. The finish reprises candy notes. If candy corn actually tasted like corn, it would taste like Eagle Rare Single Barrel. This is an excellent and enjoyable whiskey, a fine presentation, and a good value.

Yellowstone.

As a whiskey writer, I drink products like Yellowstone bourbon so you don't have to. Like so many of the bourbons available today Yellowstone is, quite literally, not what it used to be. The brand was created by J. Bernard Dant, a son of Joseph Washington (J. W.) Dant, one of the pioneers of the Kentucky whiskey industry. It was launched shortly after the National Park of the same name was established in 1872. (The label still depicts the famous geyser, Old Faithful.) Dant originally contracted with the Taylor & Williams firm to make Yellowstone at their plant in southern Nelson County. By 1903, he was the firm's president and Yellowstone had become a major brand. After Prohibition, Dant and his sons built a new, mammoth distillery in Louisville and gave it the Yellowstone name. Glenmore bought it in 1944. The distillery had a capacity of 1,000 bushels a day and its rackhouses could hold 140,000 barrels of aging whiskey. Although the company owned other distillery properties, Yellowstone was its pride and joy.

When Glenmore and Schenley merged to form United Distillers in 1992, the Yellowstone brand was sold to Heaven Hill and the distillery was shuttered for good. Heaven Hill immediately sold the brand to the David Sherman Company of St. Louis, where it remains to this day. Sherman is not a distiller. They buy bulk whiskey for their brands. The whiskey they use for Yellowstone is some of the most unpleasant you will ever taste. It is the color of straw and smells like wet plaster. Thin and watery, it burns going down, leaving a faint taste of basil and vanilla. There is no justification for a bourbon to be this bad. Yes, it is cheap, but there are more worthy choices for the same or even less money. The venerable Yellowstone name deserves better. It should be put out of its misery.

Maker's Mark.

Maker's Mark is unique among American distilleries in that it makes (at least for sale within the USA) only one product. The significance of this is that there is nowhere to hide. There is no 'good-better-best,' no extra-aged expression, no bottled-in-bond version, no line extension of any kind. According to all available evidence, Maker's makes everything they sell and sells everything they make. The fact that they use 1,000 gallon dump tanks (most others are ten times that size) tells us that the product must be extraordinarily consistent from barrel to barrel, a significant achievement.

Maker's is a wheated bourbon sold at 90 proof with no age claim. It comes in a distinctive bottle with a simple, one-color label and trademark hand-dipped red wax seal. The whiskey is not only consistent but quite good, although it has in common with other best-selling brands a mildness and superficiality that can be frustrating to more adventurous palates. But there is nothing to complain about here. Maker's is real bourbon and a completely enjoyable drink.

The color of Maker's Mark bourbon is polished brass and the nose announces that while, as the label says, the whiskey is 'fully matured,' it is only just. There is a strong sense of fresh 'white dog' lurking just beneath the mature spirit. This is not criticism. To the contrary, it makes me long for a taste of the distillery's un-aged product, which I'm sure is delicious. Both to the nose and on the tongue, the barrel's influence comes through as oak more than char. When you try to tease out different flavors you mostly get candy notes, which is typical of a wheater; caramel, toffee, even pancake syrup; the smoothness of milk chocolate with some of the bitterness of dark chocolate. One surprise: preserved lemon, which is similar to lemon candy but with more citrus edge. There is mint in the quick, clean finish.

The achievements of pioneers are always most remarkable when you consider them in the context of their time. It is striking, for example, to visit Oak Park, Illinois, where you can view a modern Frank Lloyd Wright-designed house next to a gingerbread Victorian built in the same year. In the same way, Maker's Mark bourbon contrasts sharply with the rough and ready bourbons that dominated the category when it was created fifty years ago. Although Bill Samuels Sr. did not create Maker's Mark all by himself, his was the vision; of a whiskey that while still definitely bourbon would be much friendlier and easier to drink than the bourbons he grew up with, but without being bland and soulless. Without question Maker's Mark has been marketed brilliantly, but it is axiomatic that even the best marketing can only sell a product once. After that, the product itself has to do the job and that Maker's Mark does admirably.

Bibliography.

Alexsis Lichine's New Encyclopedia of Wine and Spirits.
New York, NY: Alfred A. Knopf, 1974.

Beam, Jo Ann. *Descendants of Jacob Beam.* Bardstown,
KY: Oscar Getz Museum of Whiskey History, 2001.

Bertrand, Nancy, et. al. *Wakefield: 350 Years by the
Lake.* Wakefield, MA: Wakefield Item Press, 1994.

Brown, Lorraine. *200 Years of Tradition: The Story of
Canadian Whisky.* Markham, ON: Fitzhenry &
Whiteside, 1994.

Campbell, Sally Van Winkle. *But Always Fine Bourbon:
Pappy Van Winkle and the Story of Old Fitzgerald.*
Louisville, KY: Limestone Lane Press, 1999.

Carson, Gerald. *The Social History of Bourbon: An
Unhurried Account of our Star-Spangled American
Drink.* Lexington, KY: The University Press of
Kentucky, 1963.

Cecil, Sam. *The Evolution of the Bourbon Whiskey
Industry in Kentucky.* Paducah, KY: Turner
Publishing Co., 1999.

Collins, Richard H. *History of Kentucky.* 1874.

Crowgey, Henry G. *Kentucky Bourbon: The Early Years
of Whiskey-Making.* Lexington, KY: The University
Press of Kentucky, 1971.

Downard, William. *Dictionary of the History of the
American Brewing and Distilling Industries.*
Westport, CT: Greenwood Press, 1980.

Elliot, Sam Carpenter. *The Nelson County Record: An
Illustrated Historical & Industrial Supplement.*
Bardstown, KY: Record Printing Co., 1896.

Harrison, Lowell H., and James C. Klotter. *A New History of Kentucky.* Lexington, KY: The University Press of Kentucky, 1997.

Jackson, Michael. *The World Guide to Whisky.* Topsfield, MA: Salem House Publishers, 1988.

Kilby, Kenneth. *The Cooper and His Trade.* Fresno, CA: Linden Publishing Co., 1989.

Marrus, Michael R. *Samuel Bronfman: The Life and Times of Seagram's Mr. Sam.* Hanover, NH: University Press of New England, 1991.

Pacult, F. Paul. *American Still Life.* Hoboken, NJ: John Wiley & Sons, 2003.

Pearce, John Ed. *Nothing Finer in the Market.* Louisville, KY: Brown-Forman Distillers, 1970.

Powell, Robert A. *120 Kentucky Counties.* Lexington, KY: Kentucky Images, 1989.

Regan, Gary, and Mardee Haidin Regan. *The Book of Bourbon and Other Fine American Whiskeys.* Shelburne, VT: Chapters Publishing, Ltd., 1995.

Rorabaugh, W. J. *The Alcoholic Republic: An American Tradition.* New York, NY: Oxford University Press, 1979.

Simon, Andre L. *A Concise Encyclopedia of Gastronomy.* New York, NY: Harcourt, Brace, 1952.

Taylor, Richard. *The Great Crossing: A Historic Journey to Buffalo Trace Distillery.* Frankfort, KY: Buffalo Trace Distillery, 2002.

Index.